PRIMITIVE PSYCHOTHERAPY

By Renato Trinca

Copyright - 2016 Renato Trinca

Cover by Joseph Ventura

"The liberty of the individual is not a benefit of culture. It was greatest before any culture, though indeed it had little value at the time, because the individual was hardly in a position to defend it. Liberty has undergone restrictions through the evolution of civilization, and justice demands that these restrictions shall apply to all."

Sigmund Freud

... This book is dedicated to whoever wishes it to be dedicated to them, just to make things easier...

1 INTRODUCTION

Primitive psychotherapy was founded in 1993. Well, it has actually been around for millions of years, and I didn't invent it, Mother Nature did (or God). I only gave it a name.

This book rises from the ashes of its precedent: "Guarire la mente tornando ad abbaiare" (Ipsia Editore, 2011- translated "Cure the mind by barking again") which contained a synthetic version of "Primitive Corporeal Psychotherapy". This book is meant to create a space for its complete consideration. The common denominator of the two books is to underline the importance, or rather the lack of, our animalistic side, which has been banned by civilization but that is a present anomaly within it. Although, we can hardly call it "animalistic" since animals don't binge as much as humans, who accumulate everything.

Here, I have decided not to use the term "corporeal" because "primitive" psychotherapy must be "corporeal" by definition.

This book therefore contains 35 years' worth of observations of various psychotherapeutic approaches, as both a patient and a pupil, but also as a psychologist and psychotherapist (even at the tender age of 6 I had a side job listening to my mother's quarrels). The previous book, a collection of my notes from 1993, had a bit of an ironic tone; this one will be more "sentimental," because I'm old now.

This time around, I did not consult an Editor, in order to avoid certain "limitations". Therefore, I apologize in advanced for any orthographic or grammatical errors that would not have happened with the help of a proofreader. To make matters worse, I am also quite lazy and tend not to reread- please have patience.

This book is for everyone: for those who are patient and those who are not. The idea is for it to be comprehensible and useful to anyone, and if it is not, that will mean that I was not able to shake off all of the theorizations- often far from the way things work naturally- that I came across in my journey through *"Psicognagnola,"* as my mother, an ex farmer from Veneto (civilized in Milan) called it, meaning that Psychological theories were a way of not facing life as it really is. Not bad, poor country woman mother of mine, or perhaps, poor me?

For whoever believes that "Primitive Psychotherapy" means going back to living in caves or hugging trees, I will clarify that in order to not destroy ourselves and the planet, it is not necessary to wear nose rings and perform rain dances, but simply to reintegrate our animal side. It is a part of us that perceives what determines our survival and what doesn't; that doesn't fall asleep listening to chit chat and promises of emotional wellbeing through the acquisition of people and material things, that is in contact with fear and physical pain, which saves us from the schizoid alienation of civilized society that forces us "live" like smiling idiots while the sky is falling, both economically, psychologically and alas, ecologically (which really means: worse physical health and tons of pharmaceuticals for the zombies who can afford them).

1.1 LEGEND

1)When I speak of being "human, man, child, animal, Psychotherapist" etc. for convenience, I am always referring to both the female and male genders, unless of course it is specified.

2) Since I never liked the term "Patient," you will see it replaced by "Impatient," because I believe that it should be the Therapist that is "patient", although he is often impatient to apply his own theoretic "beliefs" to his cases in order to reach misleading "cures" that only feed his precarious self-esteem.

3) When I speak of the "civilized" human, I intend a person that is more or less conform to the moral norms indicated by the society in which they live and that does not only accept but also finds consolation in the rules that distinguish it and for whom every violation of which is cause of internal suffering (conflict with the "Super-Ego," if you prefer Freud).

4) I will use the terms "Primitive," "Animal" and "of Nature" interchangeably, referring to this type of Psychotherapy that, as I mentioned, has existed for millions of years.

5) I apologize to the ethologists if I don't consider the specific differences between species of the animal kingdom, but it is not important for the purposes of this book. The distinction is made between those who are able to carry forward their species without destroying themselves and the planet, and those who cannot, namely, Humans.

2 INTRODUCTION: THE FAILURE OF PSYCHOTHERAPY

In order to understand what "Primitive Psychotherapy" is, it is necessary to first outline a global vision of the world of psychology of the individual today and its (unavoidable) critics.

Let's start by citing two books, written by two eminent authors, James Hillman and Micheal Ventura: "We've Had A Hundred Years of Psychotherapy- And the World's Getting Worse" (1992, HarperCollins) and the second edition of the same book "We've Had A Hundred Years of Psychotherapy- And the World's Getting Worse" (1993, HarperOne).

If you don't feel like reading them, here is an excerpt of the presentation of the books: *"Although the twentieth century was the century of psychotherapy, a real industry that can count on a large number of schools and therapists and a bevy of wealthy customers, the world has not ceased to be an inhospitable place: wars, oppression, disasters ecological, ugly buildings, alienating work. The paradox is that people are being treated and the world gets worse. Too implants to ourselves and our inner life, we forget that outside, things that do not go in the world. Psychological therapy was thus transformed into a reactionary practice, while there should be a revolutionary psychotherapy, hooked to things, to the outside world, to politics."*

Still, the authors proved to be quite optimistic back then, because in 1998 things indeed started to get worse in the world. We are, in fact, witness to an increasing numbing of the population in a world where the 1% is richer (meaning it has resources for survival) than the remaining 99%. Without going too into the details, we will be discussing the quality of life, the irreversible climate and pollution of food, water and air that cause more death by cancer than all of the wars put together, the difference being that this time, the enemy is invisible.

Naturally, I'm not referring to the conditions of third world countries, but of powerful ones like the United States, Russia, Europe etc. where the great divide between wealth and poverty is growing, where the middle class is disappearing and power is constantly being concentrated into the hands of few.

2.1 WHAT DO YOU MEAN "THE WORLD'S GETTING WORSE"?

Let it be clear: this is not a lecture on eras or the denying the progress and advantages of civilization. Even in just the medical field, without such progress we would still be living as they did in the 1800's when 6 children out of 10 born died. Just consider that in the last 100 years the population has grown from one billion to seven billion, which proves a greater survival rate (although we would have to look into how, exactly). **The aim is to focus on the regressive processes of the Human animal,** which started thousands of years ago with the constant dismissal of its animal part to make space for its self-destructive part (which is not the animal part as we will see). **This process relentlessly brings us towards the alienation (and consequently self-destruction) of our species**, which lends itself to its advances in "Human" intelligence in terms of increasingly sophisticated tools for domination. This leads to a change in the world, both for those who make it happen, and those who receive "treatment." In other worlds, the first thing to be affected is the economy, which has a domino-effect on the quality of life of Humans, both from a material and physical standpoint, as well as a psychological and ecological one.

In order to obtain this, an "invisible" violence is necessary, and nowadays it is possible to disguise it, transforming it into an aggressive force that is conform to the law, that even makes choices about our physical health.

There was a time where the exact same thing used to happen, **the difference being** that the more we turn back time, the more similar we were to the Human-animal, and **the tools we had were not as damaging**; they could almost be compared to those of actual animals, that is, a possible abuse of power among peers was 1:1. A lion can only confront one another lion at a time in order to decide who will eat first. Even in a small group, Humans can give an "order" and decide not even to leave the "leftovers" to millions of people. Another example: because of the various industrial revolutions, a few gained wealth and many gained a reasonable means of survival, at least up until a few decades ago. In fact, until then it was still quite easy to find work, buy a house and have children without going into debt and being forced into an alienated lifestyle. New forms of slavery were created, and this accumulation of resources for a decreasing number of Humans required energy producing systems that were "dirty but profitable" in order to keep the air-conditioner-using, SUV-driving population under control, without the faintest clue of the quantity of radioactive waste that we have been producing for millions of years, of the GMO foods we have been eating, the effects of global warming etc.

To be clear, **I'm not saying "it's all those bad guys' fault,"** it hadn't been them, it would have been someone else, I am talking about an innate Human process that would have been done by other Humans.

If we really want someone to take responsibility, we should talk about all of the people who, for centuries and centuries, attempted to understand the Human being and find a solution to this unstoppable process, with endless theories about Humans, except the simplest of matters: the laws that regulate our nature and how they have been distorted. Hillman and Ventura ask themselves what first Psychoanalysis and later Psychotherapy hadn't done for the world to be getting worse, but I would like to expand the conversation to all of the theories or strategies that investigate the nature of Human beings, including philosophies, that have never been complete and have never brought about change, precisely because they weren't thought of by our animal parts.

The process of civilization is not possible without repressing a few aspects of our nature, in particular those tied to vitality and survival.

Obviously, I did not come to explain how the helix turns and offer solutions. As I've mentioned, I do not have theories, I have only listened to those of others and simply come to the conclusion that, in the end, the most convincing one that seems to explain everything is the theory that Nature itself speaks of, with the facts, and for millions of years. I will thus follow it until it re-inserts me into its cycle, giving me a new role as food for insects.

In order to understand what Primitive Psychotherapy is (which really everyone knows unconsciously) we must understand, or better observe the most evolved animal of all the species': the human being.

3   WHO IS THE HUMAN ANIMAL?

3.1   BEHAVIORS OF THE HUMAN ANIMAL

Considering what life was like 2,5 million years ago (the Hominids, not the Sapiens), it is easy to wonder what kind of behaviors were put into act by Humans in order to reach the point we are at now.

They must have had "instincts" so as not to become prey to some other animal, to find food, to create shelter, to combat rivals, to reproduce, to tend to lovingly and defend offspring. Without any one of these behaviors we would not be here today. We can also assume they must have found pleasure in living, otherwise they would have simply been idle, waiting for lightning to strike them in the head. As it turns out, these behaviors correspond to the category of **fundamental emotions**, without which we would not have survived.

Each of these has been **fundamental** to the **survival** of our species:

- Joy to motivate us to keep living;
- Anger or aggressiveness to attack or defend ourselves;
- Fear for self-conservation;
- Sadness, allowing us to abandon things and move forward;
- Curiosity, because without it we would never discover anything new and would therefore never find better ways to adapt to the environment.

Obviously, human offspring resisted the environment to varying degrees depending on their genes and how much they had been nourished and nurtured, exactly like any other animal. The only difference is the duration of the nurturing phase which varies from species to species.

The human never changed. Such "animal" behaviors can be seen even today (although we will see later on that it isn't exactly so), in powerful humans, as in the rest of humanity. It is an amplified scenario however, meaning that there are more sources of food, houses, reproduction etc. Such behaviors are simply **"hidden"** from our morals, yet they produce, thanks to human intelligence, devastating effects. By now empathy has become a mere projection, equivalent to the photo of a dead child washed up on the landing beach of migrants, that upsets us for a little over two days. Unfortunately, there are 10 thousand other dead bodies out there, but hey, no photo, no empathy.

The human being was sane as long as it looked more like what an animal looks like, meaning it had a biological system of self-regulation that all animals have. You will never see an animal gather more food than it needs for survival and for its offspring, or mark a vast area of territory for no real reason. Only the human animal began to do these things. Little by little, its mind became hypertrophic, capable of building "tools" for domination (with the creation of the Neocortex of course).

Later on, civilization, which became necessary because it was initially advantageous for collective survival, began inhibiting certain primitive instincts, "public" ones, which proved to be dangerous when living together. This brings us to the necessity to create religions/laws/morals, in order to self-regulate the "dangerous" behaviors - such as aggressiveness or sexuality and therefore rivalry- for the masses, and obviously not for those who were able to dominate. We have now realized what it was all for.

Naturally, most civilized Humans are not aware of its own behaviors; he must stabilize a sort of equilibrium in order to avoid conflict with himself. Another thing to consider is the way such conflicts manifest themselves in a way that the Human is not able to identify, which brings him, at times, to Psychotherapy or to follow a certain belief (which can also be a philosophy) in order to make sense of the conflict, at least temporarily. If we think about the people that we know- without being psychologists or emotionally involved with that person- we can identify their incoherencies and contradictions, but we are rarely able to notice our own. This is called being unconsciously ambivalent.

3.1.1 <u>Human ambivalence</u>

As many of us know (I think), the most common method for "hiding" certain behaviors from the moral needs of civilization- that would clearly have a negative effect on public morale and ourselves- is differentiating between "good and evil." We all naturally put ourselves on the good side, while putting others are on the bad side. This isn't very logical; if "evil" exists, someone must be doing it. If I said that "only a handful of dictators, war mongers or economic powers were the only ones doing it, and without even realizing it," you would all agree. However, if I said that us Westerners, who make up 20% of the world population, consume 80% of its resources and the other 80% barely survives and often die early, being left with only 20% of resources, we automatically become even more "evil" than the war mongers. Here things might start to get uncomfortable, because I've shed light on a conflict with ourselves that we normally and rationally keep under control with the illusions of civilization. In fact, many would say "but I'm not an assassin." In fact, I didn't say "assassin," which is a moral judgment, but that within us there is a part that is empathetic towards others, and another that is willing to abandon others for the sake of our own survival. The important thing is to not be conscious of it, otherwise it was trigger our empathetic side in the form of guilt. I know, it's bothersome just to speak of it, but in books we pretend to take action, but nothing ever really changes. Frankly, cannibalism is more "honest" and civil in comparison, but I admit that buying chicken from the supermarket is more reassuring.

3.2 THE HUMAN ANIMAL AND ITS BIOLOGY

The human animal has genes in common with very distant ancestors: fruit flies, plants and even bacteria. This is to say that we are not something in and of itself, but the "sum" (for lack of a better term) of all of the animals that have populated the earth, or as a biologist would say: "ontogeny recapitulates phylogeny," meaning our bodies are the thread of the evolution of life.

The Chimpanzee seems to share 70% (some say 98%) of the human genome, and for 15% we are even more similar to the gorilla. Basically, we are simply evolved animals, differentiated for the neocortex (the most recently developed part of the brain), language and intelligence. But if we were to surgically removed these structures, only our purely animal part would remain (from the Thalamic structures downwards).

I'll use the old model of Mclean (although today it is more common to speak of Neurotransmitters), to give a **rough idea of the correspondence** between neurobiological structures and our behaviors- although it would only really be necessary to observe them- we have three fundamental parts of the brain: the "**R-complex**", responsible for purely animalistic behaviors, which reaches about halfway down the spinal cord, the "Limbic System," which is located higher up and is characteristic of mammals and are responsible for emotional behaviors and the most recent "**Neo cortex**" that is a sort of calculator for human functions.

The poor neocortex takes orders from the other two, even though we are convinced that we make decisions ourselves, as conscious and rational people that contemplate our decisions. Yeah, right.

Whoever has been to psychotherapy (but also unofficial substitutes, that is, half the population) at least once, has gone in hopes of understanding why certain things happen or behave in a way that is undesirable, understandably wondering why, believing that he is the only one (remember that he/she are interchangeable here).

Conclusion: the big difference between Humans and other animals lies in the great analytic intelligence of the neocortex, capable of building anything, even changing the climatic conditions of the world, but always commissioned by the other two parts, that have their reasons.

Therefore, it is legitimate to ask which of the three structures is responsible for the notorious affirmation that "...the world's getting worse" (regardless of Psychotherapy) mentioned by Hillman and Ventura, that leads us to inevitable self-destruction.

3.3 THE HUMAN ANIMAL AND ITS SELF-DESTRUCTIVE PART

You might think that it is our **animal part** (R-complex, or the "oldest" part of the brain) with its primal instincts, that wins over things like empathy, compassion etc. that are so tragicomically human, and thus distinct from the ferocious "beasts." In the end, we are all dominant predators that aim to attack our rivals, anywhere and by any means necessary, in order to access wellbeing, that is, resources for survival.

You could also think that it is our **big analytic brain** (the famous "Neocortex") at the service of our primal animal instincts, that leads us to build sophisticated domination tools: weapons, dictators, false democracies, moral and behavioral obligations imposed by religious beliefs, politics and blah blah blah.

But both theories would be wrong, for a very simple reason: **animals** and **newborns** (and this goes for sane adults too) both have a body that is programed not to go beyond its own basic needs, if they do, they get stuck- and don't work very well when chubby. They don't need a thousand preys or a thousand toys, even though children nowadays look more and more like little adults, sharing the same voracity for "things."

So who is to blame? **That part of the brain in charge of emotions, called the Limbic System**, that seeks to fill "voids" in adulthood, caused by insufficient "primary nurturing," that keeps track of our most profound emotional trails, apparently making us forget them. It is obvious that the problem can be either **excessive** or **lack of** nurture. A lack of nurture creates a need to "fill" as an adult, and doesn't allow for a healthy management of resources. A silly metaphor to get the idea: if I give a kitten a small amount of milk, it will be the same as giving it continuously resulting in the kitten always wanting to fill its belly with milk. In other words, we will have "bulimic" adults that attempt to accumulate "things" in order to not feel the depression of the void, that corresponds to an emotional death (not a real one- nobody dies if he doesn't get his milk at 30 years ago, but it feels the same).

Obviously the consequent behaviors of this (socially declared) "egoistic bulimia" are in conflict with both our profound **animal part** that gets sick after overeating, and our **Limbic-empathetic part** that leaves an emotional trail of footsteps of the love we received from our parents and does not approve of being "egoistic or evil" to others.

It is obvious that **emotions** are what gives us a reason to live, but while in animals and newborns these **develop at the same pace of reality**, in the civilized adult they move (and are moved) towards goals that, once achieved, no longer have effect and thus creates a need to go to greater lengths to feel them. Basically, periods of "happiness" that get shorter and shorter.

Today we find ourselves with a great **"hunger" for emotions**. However, since they only live on air and inconsistent realities, they allow economic and power complexes to exert control over the masses, **moving the emotions towards things and people that are non-functional to our survival**, but seem to fill "a void" that will never actually be filled.

So, how do we call this **need to fill the (emotional) "void"** that makes us literally consume the world? By now everyone knows, its called **reaction or avoidance of Depression**, a sickness from which our civilized society suffers from more and more and which leads to self-destruction. Let's get to know it a little better.

3.4 THE HUMAN ANIMAL AND DEPRESSION

There are various types and degrees of depression, but until it openly manifests itself, causing one to fall into apathy, humans and society **defend themselves** from it in the same way: by distancing themselves from it as much as possible. Think of an empty sack: this is the unpleasant sensation to avoid. **How do you get away from it?** By filling it with things, false, compensating love, substances, food, ideologies, religions, money and power. These last two, when put together, allow for maximum indulgence, but as we've seen, it is never enough.

Some may believe that the rich and powerful, that is those who successfully act with their animal instincts, don't suffer from depression. However, **Depression is transversal** to the social classes and therefore affects everyone equally. Why? I've already told you the answer: in order to not feel the emptiness or the depressing sense of unease, we accumulate useless "things." A good example of this is the celebrity that has everything: love money, fans etc. but drinks and does drugs until they die from it.

Maybe we need a good **silly metaphor**: think of a child that was fed very little (or too much, it's the same if the food was only meant to hide anxiety). As an adult he will be able to eat as much as he wants, but he will never find peace or be satiated, he will simply get fatter and fatter until he explodes. You could apply the same metaphor to everything else, from cigarettes to symbiotic love, but especially to money and power, which are capable of "filling you up" with anything. This is the cause of the self-destruction of the human species. **Looking to resolve a "trauma" by denying it and compensating for it**, which is like trying to make up for someone beating you up in the past by beating up the entire world. It's a feeling that might last for a few days, but as soon as the effect wears off, you find yourself with the same humiliation of the original beating and you start all over again, until you grow old and no longer have the energy to beat anyone up anymore. At that point all of the depression that you had managed to keep away for so long comes crashing down. It may seem banal, but if you look closely, that's all there is to human history.

3.4.1 <u>Do animals suffer from depression?</u>

I'm sure you know the answer for pets, there is even a branch of Psychology for Cats and Dogs. However, even dolphins show signs of depression when they are put into an aquarium. There, their lives are shortened from about 50 years in the wild, to about 20 years when after just two strokes they find themselves running into pool tiles (it seems their natural Sonar turns off).

One might draw the conclusion that as soon as the animal is "castrated" of its functions in its natural habitat, it becomes depressed.

Studies on the depression of **wild animals, or not in captivity**, are extremely rare and subject to controversial interpretation. It's true that the famous Limbic system also exists in inferior mammals (though in a lighter version), and therefore you might think that any kind of wild pup can be nurtured badly and might consequently have psychological damage or depression. But why can't that be true? Simply because the "wild" animal world would continue in the steps of Humans.

Therefore, you cannot conclude that the inadequate nurturing of a wild pup simply leads to a physical weakness that makes it more vulnerable to life, but you will never hear of a deer that throws itself against a wall or that is apathetic, waiting for death in a corner.

Rather than actual studies, there are people that claim to have observed beached whales, dolphins that take their own lives by holding their breath and even sheep that jump off cliffs, just as there are people who swear to have seen Aliens or the Virgin Mary. We will never know if these animals commit suicide and, in that case, if it was caused by depression, but it doesn't really matter here. In the animal kingdom, survival of the fittest rules and I repeat, **the system works without humans**. In the human kingdom, on the other hand, we have the problem of self-destruction of the entire system, humans and planets alike. That does matter.

3.5 THE SOCIAL AND POLITICAL HUMAN ANIMAL

We need a Psychotherapy *"of things, of the outside world, of politics"* said Hillman and Ventura. But why wasn't this possible?

The human animal requires a lot of time and nurturing before it reaches autonomy; for many years, its survival has depended on others and this has made it **very fragile**, even at an adult age and although most of the time they are unconscious of this, it has visible effects.

It is not a coincidence that from the dawn of time, humans have **invented divinities of various forms, and have always asked them for protection**, at times even sacrificing their life in hopes of attaining a better one or continuing to live through their offspring (something that also exists for animals, that genetically follow their mission of continuing life on earth).

As mentioned previously, it is inevitable that in this delicate period of nurture the so called **"voids"** are created, especially nowadays with the sort of virtual nurturing that has come with the invention of television, internet and parents who work three jobs just to be able to buy a house. If the "void" comes with **high analytic intelligence**, but **lacks emotional intelligence**, we will have an adult that has numerous occasions to take on powerful roles in order to tame it, but will never really be satisfied with everything he has. On the other hand, if the "void" comes with less analytic resources, it will be difficult for the person to come to power as an adult- unless that power can be achieved through some fortuitous gift such as being born with a beautiful voice- and thus the psychological unease will be even greater, taking the form of frustration.

Obviously there are people with more or less of a need to tame this "void," but we can say, observing society as a whole, that the vast majority of people these days are more inclined to "fill." We are all force-feeding, some more, some less and by the means available to us: food and alcohol for some and money and power (that allow us to buy almost anything else) for others. It is just an example just to get the idea across- as I mentioned already, the world is full of rich alcoholics, but no poor man has the money or power to go to rehab at a private clinic.

Conclusion: we have always lived off of this fragility/fear, that since infancy continues to grow and that requires support, nurture, security... Just look at religion, political leaders, ideologies, sects, wizards, relatively qualified physical and mental health professionals, multinationals etc...

The catch, which leads us back to Hillman and Ventura but can also be recognized up to one hundred years ago and in various fields, is that the world's data (and not just in recent years) shows that this **fulfillment of needs has always been false** and has only been beneficial to those who imposed it.

Therefore, the reason for which a Psychotherapy of the outside world, including politics, doesn't exist, is because the

Impatient and the therapist (official or not) **suffered and continue to suffer from the same "sickness,"** that is, they didn't integrate with their animal part enough which is only way of being able to **see the outside world lucidly**. How could I see it if I'm so busy stuffing myself?

Remember that even a "professional" Psychotherapist can become depressed if he doesn't feel he belongs to any particular school or orientation. However, if he does, he will have to sacrifice a part of himself in order to always be "accepted" into the specific system, that necessarily requires him to be coherent with its principles.

Let's try to observe our world as an animal would. Take a Wolf for example, an animal that has always been hunted and even accused of bringing back luck. He would undoubtedly observe without moral bias or judgment and without getting too involved because it would be of no benefit to him.

3.5.1   <u>What would a Wolf think of human politics?</u>

A Wolf, looking at our world, would simply say that politics do not exist. Elections, presidents, populations, nations etc. are merely the products of civilization meant to politely screw over your neighbor, apparently without using violence, so everyone is happy. In his observation, the Wolf would simply limit himself to say that the fact is there are very few powerful Wolves, though many believe to be because they stand under the same flag, which makes them proud, but the fact is they only have crumbs and even those depend on the few Wolves that have the means to ration them.

He wouldn't see the sense of wars, since there has always been enough food and resources for everyone, and would therefore conclude that there are simply some people that like to take more "food" (and resources) without using it for some odd reason.

Looking at us, he wouldn't understand why the Russian, American, European, Arab etc. populations exist, he would only see that a few Wolves of any given nationality allow many other wolves to exist within their borders providing means for survival that are more or less acceptable, but that always depend on the Wolves in power. If you told him that Putin defends the Russians and is against the Americans he would look at me like a fool, saying "but the strong (rich) wolves don't even make war amongst themselves, each of them is the head of a pack and eats first, why should he be angry with another head of a pack in America, Europe, or the Middle East, that also eats first and has a pack to keep their distance from? I understand that if the powerful Wolves didn't have enough to eat, then they would really start to quarrel, but since they do, the real enemies are the hungry wolves of their country that need to be kept on a leash- they will make war amongst themselves when they don't have enough to eat." How could you deny it? It's the facts, whatever the Nobel economists, the Media, conspiracy theorists and paranoids say. It's all there, we just can't see it because our animal part is sleeping.

3.5.2   <u>What would a Wolf say about human leaders?</u>

He would be quite perplexed, wondering "but why follow a person that doesn't give you immediate advantages? With us, if someone wants to be a Leader, we give him a couple of hours to show that he will feed all of us, and if he doesn't we choose someone else. You all chose people that not only tell you to wait, but then doesn't even catch anything- why don't you replace him right away?" The ignorant Wolf couldn't possibly understand that we are more foolish than a Pavlov's dog and when the lunch bell rings we always run to our masters, even if lunch isn't there. All it takes is a small intermediary reinforcement, say giving us a sliver of taxes with one hand and raising the service tax with the other, to make us run at the sound of the bell for years.

Differently from the studies on classic or operating conditioning, the Human seems to be quite the opposite, with all its intellect, falling for it much more than an animal. It would also be difficult to explain that it is our notorious **hunger for emotions** that cloud our view of reality.

If I made the Wolf read our history, pointing out the positive Leaders that led us to improve the human condition, he would laugh in my face. He would say that in his world, there is no improvement without autonomy and independence. He would ask me "what is slavery?" and if I told him that it was the submission of another human whose right to life or death was controlled by another, making him work for nothing in exchange if not survival, he would ask me naïvely "ah, but what do you call that now?" For him, a Wolf that cannot express his nature is a slave; in his world, even the Wolf at the bottom of the hierarchy is a free Wolf.

He would also notice that even the Leaders that preach equality are still Leaders in the end, meaning they are always in a position of dominance with respect to the others and have advantages that those who follow him do not.

In effect, the temporary wellbeing that a positive Leader brings is only the unknowing preparation (although we would have to discuss how "unknowingly") for the discomfort to come. Just look at what happened after any advantage was brought to the masses by a Leader.

I think Napoleon was right when he said that "A Leader is a merchant of hope"- at least in the human kingdom. In the animal kingdom, the head of the pack continues to be such only as long as he brings advantages, they are not in the business of hope.

3.5.3   <u>What would a Wolf say about Human work and love?</u>

In general, we can say that human work and love have continued to lose their original function belonging to the most archaic part of the brain. Both functions were "normal" until they had a logical role in the economy of survival. Today we are witnessing an increase in our subjugation of these "fetishes," that have also become subject to emotional compensation of our past frustrations.

One thing is to have a job that gives a sense of dignity and meaning to our existence, that correlates to the possibility of procuring the food of our ancestors, another is to spend 15 hours a day sitting at a desk in order to earn goods that we don't need and that only cause us to be obsessive, constantly looking for more.

You could say the same for love, the closest and most direct promise of "fulfilled nurture." Precisely because it became a sort of revenge over an unchangeable past, by attempting to compensate with "quantity." Here too we seek to "drown ourselves in love" and other fulminating emotions, that usually get consumed quickly in order to seek out other apparently "more nourishing" ones. This produces offspring that gets weaker due to the trauma of the premature separation from its parents and is thus too psychologically fragile to reproduce in a way that encourages the continuation of our species.

The Wolf that observes us will then ask: "it is as if once you catch a prey, you just leave it there and chase after another, or as if you put in the effort to mate but then forget about it… doesn't that leave you hungry and full of desire?" "Yes" should be our answer.

Love and work for the Wolf are an exchange in real and emotional terms. He would never be able to understand why people get emotional without reason, he would simply look at us and ask "why?"

A Wolf has it written in its genes. It "falls in love" only when it is to his advantage, and us humans once did the same. How can we be sure? If the ones that had nurtured their offspring with love hadn't been naturally selected, then we wouldn't be here.

I can also add that in my line of work, it is known that panic attacks have been widely recorded in the last 35/40 years, coincidentally right around the time when television, then internet, the increased cost of buying a house etc. forced parents to have to work 40 jobs, delegating cold tools with no empathy to raise their children, making them insecure and overly attached to material objects, which have become their real parents. These "cold" objects, consequently made the children cold too, desensitizing them to the lack of affection, and warming them with psychoactive substances and false love that is consumed in a heartbeat or that remain eternal because they are never really achieved (given they don't commit suicide first). I remember a case (not one of mine, but in the newspapers) of a 14- year- old boy that took his life because he had gotten a bad grade at school and the father had taken away his Playstation. You can see immediately that that toy had temporarily (though it had been sufficient) his only reason for living (or false form of nurture).

Therefore, we shouldn't be surprised if this schizoid type of "empathy," that appears and disappears, leaving behind nothing but ice, causes an increase in cases in which children hack their parents to pieces without feeling the slightest remorse at that moment. Just think of how often we read about Humans that shoot into a crowd that has become the object of hate in their imagination, but has no real connection to reality. Aggressiveness in animals and in the animal part of the Human surely exists, but always has the objective of a real possibility of survival. Now, however, it has become the projection of the alienated human.

I forgot to mention that today, work- excluding being a server to those who are better off than you, like the Mexicans in California- is only available to a few. On the one hand we find our sane side, that attempts to "hunt" to survive, but on the other we find a sense of impotence caused by unemployment, that causes an even greater interior distress, since without the container of "work," Humans search for that container in apparently nurturing things (drugs, gambling, children that can't be raised etc.).

The future? We are seeing it and even the Wolf could tell us without reading a newspaper: the European, American etc. middle class that has already consumed all there is to consume and no longer has the capability of cleaning toilets, will leave room for the billons of humans of the so-called "emerging" populations, ready to work 15 hours a day to have a 50 inch flat screen TV. The big catch that the powerful ones that sell the TV's haven't seemed to consider is that it is no longer possible to produce tons and tons of non-recyclable things. The planet is on the verge of collapse, but those sick with bulimia haven't even thought to find another planet to escape to once the Earth and the Oceans are nothing but a dump (and it seems they already are given that the pollution has already caused much of the fish to disappear).

4 REACTIONARY VS. REVOLUTIONARY PSYCHOTHERAPY

Citing Hillman and Ventura again: ***"... psychological therapy has transformed into a reactionary (or "counter-revolutionary") practice, while what would be necessary is a revolutionary psychotherapy of things, the outside world and politics."***

Unfortunately, it was not clarified in the book how exactly to achieve this (or how it would have been achieved). It would seem I would explain it to you, but really Mother Nature will, as usual. I challenge anyone to say that anything written in here is mine, aside from the cover (which actually isn't even mine, it's a photo taken by my good friend Joseph Ventura).

4.1 WHAT SHOULD PSYCHOTHERAPY BE GOOD FOR?

If I go into **psychotherapy, I expect** to be freed of my ghosts and act in a way that allows me to obtain adequate conditions for survival, both materially (physically) and psychologically, just as an animal would. Yet, regardless of fact that the industry of healing people, medication included, is flourishing, people are getting worse, and their anxiety has been diverted to whether or not to buy the iPhone 18 or if someone else should.

The more we perceive discomfort without identifying it, the more we rush to find solutions that only benefit those who propose them to us. Who hasn't been promised some kind of psychological and material improvement perhaps by means of beating your head against a rock, DVDs that make you live till 106, fried fish capsules, chromo therapy, breathing exercises etc.? Not to mention the American pragmatism about the power of the mind. If they worked, all we would need is word of mouth to spread some "self empowerment" that would eliminate bad luck. **Especially by following** any kind of "institution" such as a political/religious/cultural ideology or even pure psychology (Jungian, Freudian, Cognitivist etc.) until you reach a symbiotic love that suffocates itself, like everything else, and in the meantime **we've missed the chance to take care of the external conditions necessary to our survival**.

4.1.1 The concept of "healing"

Naturally, those who deal with psychological wellbeing (professional or not) **take pride in a certain success rate**. But where is all this "healing" when the fact of the matter is that everyone is getting worse and **anxiety and depression are on the rise**?

Sticking to the facts, they would all be "Reactionary" healings, which is like saying if a bear is trapped in a cage at the Zoo but they give him water and food, then the Zoo brings wellbeing.

What do I do if I'm psychologically healthy, but I can't have a job, a house, a family or children?

One thing is for sure, these "disciplines" **did not bring wellbeing**, rather such "consoling institutions" have **done damage** (including Psychotherapy as the data regrettably shows), indirectly asking us to put our vigil, animal side to sleep in exchange for a **mirage of missed nurturing**, a false and temporary wellbeing that distracts us from what was happening around us. It won't be long until the effects of this will come knocking, bringing about a general sense of panic, but it will be too late even for Xanax or antidepressants. You won't even be able to take refuge in the arms of some other "savior," trying to forget the reality of the outside world, because at that point it will be reality itself that **comes looking for us.**

4.2 WHY PSYCHOTHERAPY LOST SIGHT OF THE OUTSIDE WORLD

The answer is right under our noses: humans, with their intelligence and tools (from pharmaceuticals to false "nurturing"), have **managed to control an incontrollable suffering, while sacrificing their animal part and forgetting** that our body was designed to survive pain as long as it needs to, and to **react to outside forces**. It is no surprise that the vital organs do not have pain receptors, as if Nature had said "if a vital organ was hit, it would be useless to feel pain, it wouldn't save you."

Facing the outside world requires to **feel-act** and not to **think-act**. Feeling as an "animal" would is not like thinking. Feeling actually puts us in the game, in our own bodies and with the possible consequences of our actions in reality. This means that instead of interiorizing, you feel the real fear, for example, that every warrior must experience when faced with risk. According to some, it would be much better to "**overcome**" our fears, but even a donkey knows that when you stop fearing things, you lose your "radar" and it is the best condition for destroying you in any way. The Warrior does not overcome fear, but rather lives with it, because he constantly needs it.

Today, action comes only by means of an explosion of some kind of repression, which doesn't get you anywhere. In fact, **those who act "well"** (who will also end up suffocating themselves in the end)- meaning they improve the probability of survival of themselves and their offspring- are the very few that have accumulated power and dominance over others. **Those who do not act well**, grab a gun and shoot into a crowd, which is completely useless.

4.2.1 <u>Instincts and Automatisms</u>

I've never met a Human that didn't say he "followed his instincts" and never betrayed those instincts. In any field-business, work, choices, love. Well, if that were true no one would have ever made a mistake and the world would be just wonderful. Often, **automatic choices**, made in a particular economic context, country or time period, which lead to quick and easy fortunes, are confused with **instinctual intuitions**, that might not produce anything on an economic scale but at least attempt to change the laws of civilized survival, based on immediate profits and without causing long-term damage.

Unfortunately, in defense of this discomfort, Humans tend to take note of successes and forget failures, in fear of falling into depression.

Furthermore, today, with the economic landscape changing at the speed of light and for the worse, the idiots who make millions with by just getting lucky are rarer and rarer, the jig is up. They make an example of a handful of successful start-ups, never talking about the thousands who threw away their money. It's like Trading, 95% loses but you only hear about the winners on the Internet, the others are too ashamed.

So the facts tell us that this **is not Instinct, but Automatism**, which is simply a **stereotyped unconscious behavior**, that comes to consciousness spontaneously like this brilliant idea and turns to dust. Who or what produces this Automatism that gets confused for real instinct? Since for us neurotic Humans, what we feel is what must be true, the culprit is always our dear **Limbic System** in need of redemption, the "act/screw-up" is irresistible.

Quite the opposite of the rational Human!!!! But there have been and will always be needy people that will take their own lives and ruin themselves, following some Leader/love/crusade/mission/belief etc

I repeat: in animals, and in the animal part of Humans, there is a **strong correlation between emotion and reality**, while in our society, 99% of the time there is no correlation.

4.3 REVOLUTIONARY VS. REACTIONARY PSYCHOTHERAPY

By now you should be able to understand why Psychotherapy was not a revolutionary process. I retain that even though they weren't supposed to, even wizards tried their hand at Psychotherapy, so just imagine how many of the "charismatic characters" that reside on this Earth try to- and they have many more clients than all of the world's Psychotherapists put together.

Being Revolutionary **does not mean** causing a revolution- as history teaches us- just to stuff ourselves and become reactionary, is to oppress the newer revolutions. **Here, I intend** revolutionary in the sense of following a **different type of code of living**, that being the one Nature gave us, not the product of a thousand theories and theses that in many cases would have been better to avoid writing altogether in order to save a couple of trees for their oxygen, which will soon be worth more than gold.

This code requires using the **sensorial dotes** that our good God (or Gods) have given us, including signs of satiety (and I don't mean food) that prevent us from filling ourselves with useless things. I repeat, this is all just chit-chat for me, because according to logic, and even an Engineer will understand, **if you don't want to feel things that you can't control, such as pain, then you won't sit your ass on a thorny bush either**, which is exactly what is happening in this time in history.

4.3.1   How did all of this happen?

That is, how did Humanity (Psychotherapy, I repeat, had just a minor role) become reactionary and not revolutionary? Excluding those poor guys that try to keep a primitive revolutionary mindset but are destined to succumb to modern technology.

Perhaps I can explain it better with a metaphor: I'll use the Wolves that live (or lived) in the wilderness of Siberia, but I could also use the people of emerging countries that are only now discovering our world and are abandoning their sane animal part, because they don't have anything to eat (because we took it from them, ha ha), or the Occidental populations when they were made of poor immigrants, fazed by the World Wars. Although, it must be clear that the big "mess" of Humanity was made thousands of years ago, but at the time without irreversible consequences.

Let's go on; I come to these Siberian Wolves (civilization) and I take one of the elders and one youth. I bring them home but I put them in separate rooms, where I give them food and water, heating and a bed to sleep in. Each one has a small garden, but it's made of concrete and deodorized to throw off their sense of smell. What do I get? By anticipating their needs, I deprive them of all of the endowments that nature gave them in order to see to those needs and survive (including rebelling or setting themselves free). It will be much more difficult to deprive the elder Wolf who had lived a certain way for years in Siberia, and would likely try to attack me and escape every time I entered the room. I would however be able to do so with the younger Wolf, who didn't have time to apply his innate capacity to perceive and respond to the natural world. After living in my apartment where everything was given to him, if I brought him back to Siberia he wouldn't last a day. Terrified, he would then beg me to bring him back to my apartment, thinking he wouldn't be able to handle life in Siberia: the pain, the exhaustion, but the joy and liberty too. He's trapped, his future is in my hands and I can do whatever I want with it, I could keep him alive so long as he is useful to me, or I could do away with him lawfully so that none of the others start to panic.

So, if I can make a Wolf pup give up his nature in exchange for manipulated nurture, I could most definitely do so with a child. I could take away his vitality within his first year of life, he wouldn't even be able to be a "wannabe" (unconsciously, of course) student revolutionary from the 60's. There are wealthy parents that come to Child Psychotherapy saying "This is my son. He's just 5 years old but speaks like an adult. He is extremely intelligent, but he has some problems…" You'd look at these children with the same eyes that betrayed the poor wolf pup, but that didn't have anything to do with the rational arguments of which they were made subject. We would play ball with them and I would continue to block them until they were raging mad and started to hit me ☺. Only after months of being able to physically express the wolf pup they had never been able to be- the adults are basically frozen at this point, the story is actually much longer and difficult- they would melt and hug you with tears in their eyes, and do you know what would happen next? The parents would take them away, because now that they were "sane" it was no longer useful to their unconscious need for affection.

4.4 HAS REVOLUTIONARY PSYCHOTHERAPY EVER EXISTED?

Revolutionary Psychotherapy in the animal kingdom (and cavemen) has always existed. There is no animal (besides the ones domesticated by humans) that hesitates to express any kind of tension that it is experiencing, only Humans are taught to hold it in. *This* is their psychotherapy; **"they heal"** **in every moment**, simply by expressing their unhappiness or discomfort with an action that eliminates the external source of stress, that is constantly being monitored with the senses. **The outside world is everything to them**, even when their internal world has made them weak (due to lack of nourishment or affection as a pup). Imagine teaching a cheetah how to stretch its muscles- first he'd eat mine, then he'd stretch his own.

It doesn't matter if the animal isn't able to eliminate the external problem (they don't have the weapons of the human mind) but they try with all their might, fighting for survival without acting with automatism as we do. There is no room for useless thoughts, they'll attack anything for the sake of survival, and when they get to the famous "learned helplessness" (Seligman, I believe) they immobilize in order to save energy in case the situation becomes favorable, their last resource for survival. According to experiments on learned helplessness in animals, when the animals understood that there was no solution, they didn't leave their cage, even though the commotion had stopped. In my opinion these studies are a bit off because of the fact that they were animals in captivity. A wild animal would realize when the external conditions had changed, otherwise they would have all become extinct for lack of adaptability (this is a personal opinion of mine).

I would recommend taking a look at Peter Levine's studies on the elaboration of trauma. There is also a video (I hope there still is) of a Bear that discharges the tension of fear after being put to sleep with a shot of anesthesia. The Bear is a metaphoric example of the Revolutionary Psychotherapy that never came to be: as soon as the outside conditions are right, he reacts.

4.4.1 <u>Why is this only possible in the animal kingdom?</u>

Because the animal kingdom does not possess our intelligence (we're talking about analytic intelligence, not emotional intelligence), and therefore **is not capable of building tools for dominating others**. A lion can catch a gazelle using a huge amount of energy, but it can't beat a thousand humans with weapons, the Media (internet included), dictatorships, false democracies, consensus strategies or dissuasion.

As a result, its body's system of auto-regulation is not altered as ours is by a "deviated" Limbic System. A socially repressed system that, unable to release tension in any other way, pushes us to devour four cakes that are completely unnecessary if not to slow us down and make us die faster, filling just one void that is our own grave. Or worse, we pretend to release tension with the collection and possession of resources that we don't need and on which we ultimately choke.

Animals feels emotions, but as I said, they aren't distorted as human emotions are, and thus have no need to fill any "Limbic" void by eating 200 lambs or building refuges from atomic bombs or having "bunga bunga" parties. They release tension- whose original form is always bodily but for neurotics becomes mental suffering- with three classic behaviors: fight, flight and freeze (playing dead in case of an attack as a last resort, quite the contrary of learned helplessness). The rest is a **continuous Psychotherapy** that stabilizes wellbeing through small and large body movements every time energy is in excess with no use.

An animal's anxiety of a "void" is simply for the one in its stomach every day. When it manages to take a bite out of something it's all set for the day, it doesn't plan in front of a computer for ten hours. Just look at what happens when an animal is domesticated by the human that offers it food, heat and protection, inhibiting its reactive instincts from "pain"- it loses a bit of its animal-ness and begins to suffer from depression just as we do.

The price to pay for someone's vitality, in exchange for avoiding suffering (but also happiness) is **depression**, which, if I may, also includes a reduction in the functionality of the **immune system**.

You might tell me that they live longer, but I would like to see how many of us would accept being castrated/sterilized (so they don't get tumors) so that we could live longer. With some time we will accept it, with just a bit of patience.

4.5 REVOLUTIONARY PSYCHOTHERAPY FOR HUMANS

It could exist, but not in terms of "changing the outside world". As I said, it's **too late**, we are stuck in an all too powerful system. It is exactly like asking the animal kingdom if it can save itself from the Humans that destroy it- it can't. The animal kingdom does not have the means, it's life is surrounded by a world of omnipotent Zombie Humans. The only thing we can do is to **die living rather than already dead**, like the animals do (just trying to lighten things up).

Among the Official approaches to Psychotherapy, Alexander **Lowen's Bioenergetic Analysis** is the one that **most closely resembles** the liberation of vital (therefore animal) energy from the body, drawing on energetic concepts that derived from the various oriental disciplines of the relationship between mind and body. Lowen was a student of Reich, who had been a student of Freud. As far as changing the outside world, he was born too late (although Reich had also attempted some social endeavors). It had already been some time that the economic organization controlled the politics of our advanced societies that are now capable of repressing any type of revolution unless it is needed to reinforce the status quo, something we now know is fully possible thanks to intelligence services.

Bioenergetic analysis was long considered the "strongest" therapy, in that it used various body positions and highly stressful physical exercises with the aim of freeing the vitality that was locked within tight muscles and restricted breathing.

As we will see however, **it was Lowen himself to declare his own fallacy**, consequently leaning towards ideas that brought him closer to Rogers, Maslow, Bowlby etc.

4.5.1   <u>The Bioenergetic Analysis of Alexander Lowen</u>

At age 18, my education began with Bioenergetics, first as a patient, then as a Psychology major enrolled at the School of Training in Bioenergetic Psychotherapy (SIAB). I have to admit it took me a good ten years before I realized what exactly I was doing.

Bioenergetics, was "invented" by Lowen (and Pierrakos, to tell the truth), who, like many others, preached the importance of our animal part, though he did so by attaching it on to "his" theory.

Sooner or later we will have to surrender to the fact that the only theory of the wellbeing of people is the one nature has upheld for millions of years, and that us Humans, fueled by our usual and insatiable "bulimia" of the Limbic System have always attempted to have "our own" theory in order to obtain the success and popularity necessary to spoil ourselves properly. I recommend reading Biographies and Autobiographies of the great Analysts, before their actual works- you will understand much more of what I've just said.

If someone has something to say, all he needs is one book, not one hundred. This is the first thing that struck me as a young man who wanted to become a good little Patient with the dream of then becoming an omnipotent Bioenergetic Analyst, healer of the sickness' of others.

I abandoned it precisely because the codified movement of the exercises (done several times a week for years) did not convince me. Even if I screamed, cried and suffered as "promised," something didn't add up for me, someone who grew up in public housing where physical liberty was everything and it filled your lungs with air. Then I realized what I had gained after being there for over ten years: the nurturance I had never received as a child. It's just a shame that I had to pay for that nurturance by betraying my body, my animal side, in order to please my emotional Limbic side that would have paralyzed the rest of me. Speaking of nurturance, if you have time, read Bowlby's work on attachment, that is what nature has been telling us for millions of years.

I'd like to share something that Lowen himself said at the twelfth Biennial Congress of Bioenergetic Analysis in 1994.

"Forty years have passed since I developed Bioenergetic analysis from the analytic concepts of Reich with the intention of elaborating the analytic work and expanding the corporeal procedures in order to make therapy more effective. I focused my attention on breathing, the expression of sentiment and the sexual abandon of love that manifests itself in the orgasm reflex. This program contained a great promise for all of us that were involved in

the development of this new approach. We believed that this way, we could help people reach complete fulfillment.

It saddens me to admit that Bioenergetic Analysis did not meet such expectations: as a founder and guide I feel responsible for this failure, which was due to my inadequate understanding of the profundity of the pathology that distresses the human beings of our culture. This failure also derives from my selfish determination to attain results. But for me, the last forty years were not spent in vain. I faced the arrogance and compulsiveness of my personality and I learned to accept life and let it be. This brought me to a brand new understanding of therapeutic duties and the process of Bioenergetic Analysis. I've called this new understanding 'surrendering to the body'. The end of surrender is to experience joy".

Furthermore, Lowen begins to speak of the importance of the relation and attunement (synchronization in interaction "invented" by Stern) between therapist and patient (meaning communication between animal parts that dates back to the times of Noah).

He also says: *"At the base of every existential problem there is a lack of love and unconditional positive acceptance and it is from here that healing must begin"*. To call it "nurturance that nature has made all of the animals do for millions of years" was banal. Which brings us back to the idea that we only hear things that Leaders say best, unfortunately.

In fact, if that particular day Lowen had had a fever and had told me ***"oh just cover for me and make it quick"***, I would have said: *"Guys, I was just kidding, I needed to 'cause I felt lame and I had to come to terms with an inescapable void; I could have also told you that if I pointed a gun at someone's face he would stop breathing and his muscles would contract, but I couldn't write 17 thousand books and not have everything that I had, including the Ranch. What I mean to say is, I thank you for the money I earned from those books and the therapy that you went through, but only now looking at the Empire that I build I realized that in exchange I only "nurtured" you, and I mean that metaphorically, given that you didn't become me. In reality only the body knows what's right, only our animal part that, if it hasn't been nurtured as a child, will be a nightmare for the Therapist that will, or attempt to, nurture him. I'm sorry, the only theory of wellbeing and the healing of the self belongs to Nature; we can only observe it and take a few of it's parts while stealing its Copyright."* It has a whole other effect, right? Forget about the applause and commotion, I would still have plates in my joints for the beatings they would have given me, oh, ungrateful humanity…

I repeat that we are all in good faith, Lowen included, it's just that we tend not to account for the Human (Limbic) ambivalence I explained earlier

5   PRIMITIVE (OR NATURAL) PSYCHOTHERAPY

Before getting to the point, I'll briefly summarize so that we have a nice foundation.

5.1   AN ALTERNATIVE SUMMARY

If all goes well, a human pup will find an adequate environment that responds to its needs. This will make sure that its faith in the world (meaning its possibility of survival with dignity) is high, and thus the difficulties that it will face in its physical and psychological development will not be a great burden, **because "it knows" that things have gone well in the past.** It will become an adult both physically and psychologically and will venture out deep into the world- it knows that even if once he had to wait for "milk" for over an hour, in the end it came. However, even if this initial phase of life goes smoothly, the first problem, which we will examine, is something that everyone goes through, to varying degrees.

First problem: the newborn's genetic dotes and its "profound" instincts will collide with the rules of civilization that its parents pass on to them to a greater or lesser extent. It is obvious that nurturance being equal, both an animal and a newborn would transform all of this knowledge into action, and then we could all say good night to civilization. Wild animals do this, thus no problems are created, they express everything. If we take the fundamental emotions that humans used to survive: anger, fear, sadness, joy and curiosity, it becomes clear that the process of civilization must necessarily limit some of them, and if they aren't they get us in trouble. On the other hand, if they are inhibited too much, they cause psychological problems. Imagine if at 3 years old, a child was "invited" to not try one or more of them, **with the implicit assumption** that it was the necessary condition for nurture (survival). Silly examples? "be good, don't be scared, don't try, you only did what you had to, stay in your place." Obviously **it's not as if those emotions just disappear**, if we go back to observing human behavior you can notice all of them, more or less hidden, camouflaged, justified. In fact, you will never find a dictator that doesn't believe to have killed for the good of his people, a war that wasn't the will of some God (but we take the heat for it) etc. The funny thing is that no one is lying, they really feel that way, because **all of the emotions that we feel, as twisted and detached from reality they may be, are real to us.**

Second problem: this one, in addition to the first (which applies to everyone), only applies to **those who were not able to find an adequate human environment**. Examples? A mother that consumed psychoactive substances while pregnant, transmitting them to the fetus and turning him into an addict, thus making the growing process and autonomy nearly impossible, absent fathers, pedophiles, violent people etc. Warning: these are all extreme examples to get the point across, but don't think that discreet "psychological manipulation" doesn't do as much damage. All of the inadequacies that parents had experienced in their childhood are reflected onto their children. The ones that are worse off develop Psychiatric problems (strong psychological disturbances that compromise function in various areas of life) and in many cases are "cured" with Pharmaceuticals (which are symptomatic, they don't cure). Those who are less worse off live a more or less distressing life, searching for a solution, at times seeking out professionals (Psychotherapists), at times other "authorities" that guarantee solutions and salvation via bank transfer and the unconditional adherence to their rules.

Third problem: this one causes the **greatest damage to Humanity**. The subject is born into a more or less adequate environment, but someone or something, a relative, an intermediary nurturer, a genetic dote such as beauty, a particularly harmonious voice etc. allows them to reach a **position of power** in life. Naturally there are various levels, from those who become stars and then die of an overdose, to whoever invented sunglasses with curled ends, builds an empire but spends his life accumulating things, without ever enjoying anything and have disastrous romantic relations. Think of Donald Trump, someone who- as he has said himself- "beat" depression (as if it were an outside enemy); he earned money, power, met women, had children and instead of stepping aside to enjoy it all, had to find a way to control (own) the world with political power.

The worst ones are those who have excellent analytic intelligence (I have some doubts about Trump but he does have the charisma to sell to those who don't know any better) combined with an insatiable need to tame the void that we have so often mentioned to escape depression (Napoleon's infancy is practically a manual). These people conquer the world, leaving the desert behind, stepping over bodies without missing a beat and often, in order to appease the empathetic and emotional Limbic system, giving a couple million dollars to some charity to balance out their guilt. **I hope it is clear** that genetically speaking we have a sane, emotional side that is empathetic (**that I believe is not really that closely tied with the Limbic system, but is much more archaic**) in some situations, for example with our offspring, because it not, how would they ever survive?

Conclusion: humans never changed their behavior, they are seemingly the same as that of animals, obviously hidden and unconscious for wanting civilization. But why only "seemingly"? Because the Limbic system, due to the previously mentioned problems, transforms such behaviors- that on their own wouldn't cause any more damage than they do in the animal kingdom- into greed/bulimia that is never satisfied, that destroys everything (often irreversibly) and eventually themselves. This is because our evolved emotional system (we have another more animal-like one that is hidden but much wiser) that we identify for simplicity with the Limbic system. During infancy it acts as a sponge that absorbs and records everything, both pleasure and frustrations.

As adults we then act unconsciously under its influence, thinking all the while that we decide everything ourselves. Where do you see its effect? In the human world, that is made of behaviors inclined towards useless accumulation, fueled by the famous "holes" to fill, a compensation strategy that doesn't work as adults, because, as explained earlier, if I surpass my capacity for "digestion" or management of information, affection, thoughts, works, omissions etc. of my natural system, I simply choke until I explode. If I don't explode thanks to medication, then comes the depression that I so anxiously tried to avoid with all of my useless "toys." Let it be clear that even the "poor" are not exempt from these mechanisms, it's just that instead of accumulating "things," they accumulate "small things" such as addiction to something or someone, that are more accessible to them. Furthermore, the internalizations of the Limbic System also contain a sense of guilt (such as the fear or abandonment) in case we were to rebel too much against the emotional revenge we received as a child, by disobeying and being too "selfish." Therefore, Humans must "compensate" for their "bulimia" by asking forgiveness and attempting to repair (mostly faking it, given the results) the resulting damage of their greed that, I repeat, has little to do with our animal part.

So how did the operators of mental health, professional and not, answer to such ruination? To quote Hillman and

Ventura's book- but I only because if I said it myself it would seem like I'd woken up with my ass on my head- you infer that all of the forms of healing of psychological distress (especially those not qualified to do so) have failed, but the world could have told us that before the two authors did.

So let us come to the heart of the book: what would (and has done over centuries) the Natural Psychotherapy do? Otherwise known as "primitive" because I like to remember a time when Humans looked more like animals rather than idiots…

5.2 Requirements for Natural psychotherapy

Let's go back to our silly metaphor (extreme yes, but just to get the point across) about the Siberian wolf pup taken from Siberia and put into my apartment to "civilize him" a bit, hence interrupting the nurturance of his natural pack. Let's say I was able to "domesticate him" a bit, forbidding him from certain behaviors. At the least it will make him neurotic like I am. Then I get the idea to "cure him," with my big brain that had done so much studying- I even know about animal Ethology- I've read everything there is to read. The reason why I will never be able to is written between the lines: **he has just one "system," the animal one. I have two, but I only use one of them, the wrong one**, the rational one that learned to inhibit the animal one. I could give him a bunch of consoling "prizes," as much food as he wants, females and males to mate with, but he will always be a "lame" and depressed wolf. **In order to really treat him with Natural Psychotherapy** I would at least have to be like Werner Freund (the 78-year-old man that lived with wolves, look him up), who raised lots of wolf pups. He probably read a lot of books too, but this guy was on knees, ripping the flesh off their prey with his teeth with the other wolves, behaving like them. He was one of them, meaning that he was in tune with his animal part and acted accordingly. **In these last few lines I've already said everything there is to say**, for those who have understood. For the deaf, I'll add that you can't "cure" a human being without curing both of his parts, and **if I myself had hidden a part of me from another part of me, I can only act as a "consoler," only pleasing my civilized part that will praise me, but that in the long run will kill the other part, the animal part, by depression**. This is the reason why, often, after years of therapy, we find ourselves unchanged, the same as before.

Acting this way, I would be making a mistake. I would be using a reactionary Psychotherapy, that **combats the revolutionary animal part of myself and my patient.** The results are exactly what happens in the world: the more society distances itself from the animal part of Humans, the more depression will continue to be on the rise (because the Limbic void is untamable), especially in but not limited to civilized countries, given that everyone aims to mimic our model of false wellbeing.

5.2.1 <u>Almost like Pet Therapy</u>

Put like this **it would seem like the most simple Therapy in the world**, and in fact, it is. Nature has few laws, well just one indisputable one really, that can be summarized in a few words: it is inclined towards survival and thus life, avoiding its destruction, unlike civilized Humans. It is clear then that a similar therapy is **all the more difficult to practice, the more distant I am from my animal part**, which prevents me from perceiving the actual state of sanity of my Impatient.

How do you think **Pet Therapy** works (therapy through bonding with real animals)? The closer I put a human and a real animal together, the more the human is put into contact with its own animal part. Since you can't really have a rational conversation with a Horse, you have to use another kind of code, that we also possess, that comes with the essence of our profound and vital animal part. **Furthermore, animals act like animals, legitimizing what the Limbic System considers dangerous**. It makes you feel guilty and risks feeling that sense of distance and abandon (not real but psychological, given that he might be 50, obviously). The naturalness of the animal recalls the same animal naturalness that lies within us, until it begins to effortlessly melt away the sense of guilt and thus resistance to change, **because the animal shows us that its ok to live without following the blackmailing and guilt-inducing rules that have brainwashed us** (with the usual reference to the Limbic System).

Pet Therapy is clearly a limited example, given that if the Impatient is a fully developed adult, the Therapist will have **make use of words**. The more the Impatient is neurotic and civilized (in the castrating sense of the word), **the more the Therapist will have to make him believe that he is too, in order to console him, while subtly** (in a nonverbal way) **he will have to send animal messages to the animal part** of the Impatient, without letting his civilized and neurotic side notice.

5.3 HOW DO YOU PRACTICE NATURAL PSYCHOTHERAPY?

What I'm about to write is useless, in the sense that if you believe that reading it means being able to do it, then I haven't explained myself clearly. It will only help you (both Impatient and Therapist) to know what an "animal Therapist" should do.

The Therapy of Nature does not guarantee the victory, success or survival of anyone. It simply says that in order to be well, you must act according to what's written in your neurobiology, and not in books. **That this is the best way to survive. It is the result of the biological intelligence of our bodies over millions of years, and there is no theory or computer that can match it,** if not swapping it with a photocopy of life itself, the one we rot with day after day. Mother Nature is right, because anyone who responds with the conquests of Man, would be reminded of their irreversible nature- not only ecologically speaking- put into action by man and that are reducing the possibility of a future (you might say "for many" but in reality our most recent analysis' concern everyone, unless Pluto happens to have air conditioning).

Unfortunately, by now, even for a real Wolf, the idea of survival with Humans in the way is impossible, but that's aside the point: **he will continue to be a Wolf until they beat him. He isn't conflicted with himself- as I mentioned – but with the outside world, and this is what fulfills him, even if it costs him his life.** He does just as a little mouse does when cornered: he does what needs to be done, even though there is a one in a billion chance of getting away with it.

Remember not to confuse the little Mouse with the idiot who opens fire into a crowd or decides to blow himself up; the idiot just thinks he's in a corner, he has no other cards to play, while the Mouse doesn't- he's like the migrant that risks his life on a raft, if life is impossible in his country, he really is in a corner, but if he leaves attracted by the consumerism of our society, he'll die of neurosis caused by the civil "I would like to, but I can't."

Let's examine what an "animal" Therapist should do then, and that is certainly not unlike what an animal does with its pups (don't start to think of vertebrates or invertebrates, the result is always the same: life).

The Therapy of Nature is composed of a number of parts that, as I mentioned earlier, are one thing when read, but another when done. The same difference lies between a photo of a steak and the steak about to be eaten by a Cheetah: the photo doesn't taste like anything.

I'll warn you: **don't ask yourselves every five minutes how to get in touch with your animal part, it's written later on.** It's difficult, even scary in the beginning, and not possible to control with the ego but with our biological intelligence, that is millions of years old and thus much more reliable than we are when we're rational and thinking.

Let's begin:

5.3.1 <u>Syntonization</u>

When you have an Impatient in front of you, you mustn't ask, but feel: **to what degree has his animal part been repressed**? In what deviated way do his animal instincts reveal themselves as **bulimic necessities of the Limbic System? Determine the power and the fear of abandon** for having partaken (even mentally) in unacceptable behaviors according to the civilized upbringing of his parents (a sense of guilt or morale) to then determine his resistance to change.

Let us remember that, secondary and mitigated paths that appear to be moral/ideological and that justify such behaviors- often only in the stage of unconscious desire- can be identified in any case (they're called "compensations"); if you don't find them you are already in front of a case of nearly catatonic depression, and it will become even more difficult to leave space to the vital or animal part.

Obviously things differ greatly if the Impatient is five or fifty, and you will find out why later on, for now let's just say that in general the latter is already well on his way.

5.3.2   The first approach

To say it is easy: how would you behave on your way to get a dog from a kennel? It depends on his state of being; if the dog was terrified and hiding in a corner, or young and playful, or an aggressive Pit bull, would you behave in the same way? In reality its either extremely easy or extremely difficult; the animal-like sensitivity that we have deep down, would push us to take a few steps back and test the waters to see their reactions before coming closer. Here you will have understood that if I act in an "empathetically standardized" way, things might go well for my civilized part, but I would be completely ignoring the profound animal part of the Impatient.

Naturally I could establish a so-called "therapeutic alliance" with the civilized part of the impatient, reassuring him against his internal "monsters" and getting him to like me while appearing to be a "good therapist." But if I can't also communicate with the animal part, because it happens to scare me too, rest assured we will be doing quite a few years of sucking up to each other, but in reality nothing will ever change; you will have only sedated him.

Now consider a terrified lost child or saving a man in the sea that's suffered from exposure or if we really want to exaggerate, **Post-Traumatic Stress Disorder**. How does our organism work? In case of high levels of stress caused by trauma, the organism defends itself without feeling anything, **in a state of emotional paralysis** (it has also been called "combat neurosis"). Then, only once the subject is safe does all of the **anguish** come out.

What difference is there between a human adult and an animal or a newborn? **That the time that passes from the moment of "trauma" to the release of stress**, is much longer in humans and is all the more difficult, the more he is civilized.

Conclusion: it's like your first kiss, you'll never forget the first approach. The Impatient, though unconsciously, immediately realizes if the Therapist is competent or "missing something" just like him, and in many cases, this second option is the one that triggers some good old reactionary Therapy (just so we don't forget), that is, the

usual **"care taking" that cuts your legs off, but are necessary to live in the world around you.**

5.3.3 Primary nurturance

It might seem like the classic therapeutic "maternage," but the fundamental difference is that if a person with preconceived ideas or a well-studied theory on the right type of nurture (see: "too civilized" and in scarce contact with his animal code) does this, he'd only be making trouble. The right nurturance, in nature, is done **only according to the needs of the pup, not with your own, which can be transmitted even without uttering a word**.

Furthermore, here I intend **corporeal nurturance**, exactly as animals do, or some non-invasive corporeal Therapies. In other cases, namely of civilized and reassuring but false nurturance, the effects unfortunately go into the cauldron of false improvement of psychological wellbeing, that logically speaking, by not reactivating the "sensors" for the outside world, cannot communicate with the environment, that is the entire world.

5.3.3.1 In practice

As you will know, it has long been established that our future mental health is also **influenced by prenatal life**, or life in mom's belly. Extreme examples? The mother sniffed lines of cocaine or any other drug; she suffered from Panic attacks. Less extreme examples? The mother was continually exposed to loud and unpredictable noises- perhaps the husband was a hot-tempered tenor that would destroy everything in a rage, maybe even threatening her.

The result? A newborn child that's already off to a bad start. What do you do with prematurely born babies? You put them in an Incubator, which mimics the conditions of intrauterine life, so as to complete the development of the vital organs. You could say the same for **emotional development deficiency**: you should be put in an emotional Incubator. How? Exactly as a Wolf mother would do with her most fragile pup: by strengthening him with **physical contact**.

What was, or rather, what should have been in the mother's belly? A cozy environment, accompanied by comforting sounds (heart beating etc.). Since the fetus has a cephalocaudal development (from the head down), this the most stimulated part of the womb. So with your little hand, you should very calmly and delicately warm it and comfort it, putting him bed in fetal position. This should all be accompanied by some kind of rhythmic, harmonious music. Everything needs to be adequate, but what does that mean? **Here comes the hard part**, or the easy part if you feel like an animal does. It will be the animal part of the baby to tell you how much, where, how fast, with how much pressure, rhythm etc. **In addition to this**, you can simulate, by making him shake his hands and feet, the movements he made in the amniotic sac, always "feeling" when the body experiences it as a relaxing source of protection or an invasion that creates stiffness. It is this feeling that will guide you, not a manual.

Fundamental problem: as you will know, in case of perceived danger, all organisms contract themselves (ancestral stage of defense) and thus you might find an Impatient before you who shudders at the very idea of going back to that position, because if he had already experienced a series of mini traumas he would expect others. All of this won't be a problem however, if your animal part will feel his, because you will both simply do what you allow each other to do, exactly like in the example of the pups at the kennel: it is he who will tell you how much and how to come closer, and every pup is different in terms of fear and he himself will differ every second. I repeat: **extremely complicated yet at the same time extremely easy,** just look at a healthy animal as it comes closer to a newborn baby: it "feels" him every fraction of a second and automatically knows what to do, he doesn't have to think twice. **It's like riding a motorcycle in the snow**: if I "feel" all of my proprioceptors, I'll know how to regulate my balance automatically, when to brake and when to accelerate. If I think of my partner, of the bills to pay or anything else I don't feel those proprioceptors anymore and I fall. If anything similar has ever happened to you, you'll remember it, how the mind **turned off, because any other thought "distracted" you from your radar system.**

In my practice, I've had Impatients who after years of coming, wouldn't dare come close to the couch, and others that after about a year fall asleep within two minutes and the problems becomes gently waking them up when the hour is over and the next patient is ringing the doorbell. I can't tell you how many times grown men have waken up and asked, like a child, me if there was anywhere they could continue that sweet, pleasant nap. I think that in order to do a really great job, I should have 20 vacant rooms in which they can rest when they fall into this deep state, but I don't.

Don't think that an "addict" falls asleep immediately and others don't, because any addition, as you will know, becomes a trap in the long run. On the one hand, he can't live without it, and on the other he hates it because he is a slave to it, thus, in the perception between animals, such tension is felt immediately. It's also obviously that, like all pups, they are the ones that communicate, without speaking, when and how long to stay in the human emotional Incubator. When it will have done its job, putting the subject more or less up to speed, you will start to see the desire to move, to explore, to do and to make, exactly like what happens with animal pups: when they feel ready enough, they will start to go snooping around everywhere. This is an **initial reactivation of vital energy** that will need, as we will see, adequate stimulus in the future.

You will surely notice that if you are mamma Wolves, there won't be an Impatient that is dependent on you, because the more time passes, the more his reality will change and he will need you less and less for primary nurturance, and more for secondary nurturance, that is every time he needs to face a "bigger" outside challenge. This will go on until you see them even less, just as pups that are ever more self-sufficient.

Conclusion: there are those in life that have the fortune of having been nurtured well and those who have the misfortune of not having been nurtured well, with all of the possible shades of grey in the middle. The duty of the Therapist is to get in synch with the phase of emotional development and continue from wherever it had been interrupted until its completion, within possible boundaries.

5.3.3.1.1 *A small distinction between infant and adult Psychotherapy*

I really shouldn't even write it, because it should be evident that primary nurturance in a two-year-old and in a 50-year-old adult are apparently completely different. Why apparently? Because just like in Pet Therapy (just to get an idea) a Horse is always a Horse, however, in front of a child and in front of an adult it will behave differently because it will understand that one of them is a pup, and the other an adult, especially if the latter is neurotic and unsynchronized.

So, if as a Therapist, a child of three, four years comes to you, with a troubling past behind him, but that isn't yet too inhibited by the idea of "blowing off steam," expect him to perceive "great big comforting Lioness." First he'll physically release all of the accumulated tension, and then, when he feels satisfied, he'll fall asleep in the arms of the Lioness-Therapist, knowing that he didn't even leave a scratch. Obviously, the less damaged the child is to begin with, the less time it will take to unlock his energy.

In the case of the 50-year-old adult, in general the personality is much more crystalized. If the structure is solid, then it'll be a hard time taking care of him, especially if he has a mountain of repressed rage on his shoulders.

Back to the usual lecture: an animal Therapist, without thinking, "feels" every second whether the Impatient wants to "blow off steam" and if the Impatient doesn't have any particular psychiatric disorder, will use civilized ways (for example speaking badly about someone). If instead he finds the Impatient in a state of profound prostration it would be better to go into the "Incubator." I'll remind you that this is only possible if the nurturance is not obstructed by a strong fear (or paranoia) of coming closer or feeling invaded, having already felt in danger in early childhood or even in the pre-natal stage.

5.3.4 Frustration

Even a Lioness frustrates its pup, because if she let him do whatever he wanted, he would never understand limits (and thus protection) that the reality of nature imposes. If they come near a ditch, the Lioness, without roaring or yelling, but gently and steadily, takes the pup and puts him in his place until he is able to take care of himself.

The same goes for a Human pup. In the beginning, the frustration will be bearable, for example, letting the baby cry for a few minutes before giving him milk. Later on, teaching him that he can't do everything he wants to because the world isn't there simply to please him will be ever more necessary. Imagine what it means to answer to any given whim of an infant that then becomes a child and then a teenager: it means he will never be able to participate in reality, because if he sees that his desires are not answered to and that it takes energy and sweat to achieve things, **he will avoid** the frustrating reality with any expedient, and will never grow up.

The usual lecture: knowing when, how and for how long to frustrate a son or an Impatient as a thinking and reasoning Therapist will never yield results, not even with the most complicated mathematical equations. Using out animal part however, is the most simply and easy thing in the world, as it is for the Lioness; you don't think, you observe and you "feel" the pup and the appropriate behavior will come out on its own.

Us Humans obviously have the extra "problem" of the culture of appearances and therefore the degree of civilization to impose upon the child, that will later come into conflict with his animal part. A Lioness limits herself to frustrating her pup to "open his eyes to reality," so that he can protect himself and survive in the world, not because he has to belong to some sect that forces rules on him, that are often useless, given the overall results.

A Therapist should do the same.

5.3.5 The reactivation of the body's vital energy

An animal knows very well, without speaking, **the vital and energetic state** of each one of her pups. We can too, if we use our animal part in the examination of an Impatient.

This is only to anticipate the fact that the improvement of an Impatient, can be seen, just like in an animal pup, in the increased desire to move his body, to explore the environment (the world), reacting to it without destroying it, which could be a result of our sick, backwards side, not the animal one.

So, after a primary nurturance (if necessary) comes the natural phase of active movement of the pup, that, in the case of Human babies, is sometimes limited by the parents even from early infancy. **Therefore, it is completely useless to try to force a pup or an Impatient to move their body with certain exercises** or correct their breathing as some disciplines, both Psychotherapeutic and not, teach. Other than being useless it is actually **dangerous**, because it reinforces the control of the mind and thus resistance.

How, when and how much movement is decided by the organism, not by our minds. Just imagine going to a Tiger pup or a newborn baby and trying to make him move according to what a book says is perfect corporeal movement (don't look it up, it doesn't exist), rather than allowing it to move naturally on its own. To say the least, I would be preventing him his natural relief. **To please me**, he might even scream, cry, remember, or even have a so-called "**cathartic**" experience, but I can also experience that going to church, meeting a Guru, professing my love to a person from a balcony, listening to a song, watching a movie etc. These things never really changed anything, but everyone would swear that "everything changed after that time..." If you really go to see what's changed, its simply that they have a new "owner" in exchange for warmth or the usual "nurturance" that as we now know has a price to pay in terms of giving up our true nature. Changing your life doesn't mean changing location or job.

Above all, the search for a "release" by means of physical and respiratory exercise, **forces the unconscious resistances** of the individual (the Limbic system that is afraid to change, say) resulting in them rearranging themselves the next day and becoming even stronger than before, "integrating" and controlling such exercises and dismissing them for real wellbeing, while the sterile wellbeing causes impotence is taken by the Limbic System, selling the soul to this new "parish," where however the negative aspects, such as going to pray every morning at 6am (following the metaphor, obviously) is interpreted by the animal part as a limitation of vitality and thus liberty.

.

5.3.5.1 <u>So what do we do?</u>

What does a mother Wolf or an "animal" Therapist do to encourage vital movement with its pups or a blocked Impatient? They certainly don't prescribe physical exercises to do, but rather "**provokes**" them so as to obtain natural reactions. The Wolf will give her pup a little "nudge;" the Therapist, in the case of a **little** and reactive Human, as I said, makes him play, but blocking him until he gets mad and attacks. In the case of an adult, since he is stronger, you don't provoke an uncontainable physical reaction, therefore you must have a repertoire of provocations for every level and moment, even physical, but containable, that I certainly can't reveal to you here, because then my patients would know when I'm provoking them and would avoid reacting by overthinking it.

What does it take to get a vital reaction from an Impatient? Remember that the time it takes will be communicated by his animal part when he is ready, as long as you aren't "deaf." You can only indirectly offer him an opportunity (or a small provocation) that he will take when he is ready. Furthermore, remember that in the adult Impatient, you will have to be even more careful- of the fear of "rebelling" against his parents (or the resistances) that you represent and therefore the "provocation" must be appropriate considering the feared counter-reaction, that he will slowly realize that with you, differently from before, doesn't happen.

5.3.6 In nature, extra energy (or tension) is released

What do animals do when they're tense? **They release it through their muscles and/or noises.**

Humans would be no different, not even with this natural mechanism inside of us, it is only inhibited to do it in certain contexts. No one says anything if a soccer player (or any athlete) lets himself go, yelling, making faces, wild movements. Less acceptable would be if a manager did the same as his boss told him he was getting fired- he'd look insane. This goes to show how society allows for behaviors and expressions similar to those of animals, but only in certain contexts, in others they are **unacceptable and inhibited**. Where does that energy (in the form of catecholamine) end up if it doesn't have a place to go? In Humans, it stays in the body and begins to **boil**.

So, whatever tension has been activated by an emotional state, can potentially be released. **The problem**, in the case of Humans, is that **he himself, unconsciously, inhibits the release**, due to an antique fear of disapproval (and the usual abandonment/devastation). This is a type of resistance that I will discuss later on.

Naturally, small children are like animals, so at least until a certain stage- unless the parents aren't completely out of their minds- they release energy regardless of the problems imposed by civilization.

5.3.6.1 <u>And how do Humans release energy?</u>

There are a thousand different methods that promise stress relief: from the gym or doing sports, to the innumerable body, visualization, therapeutic techniques etc. So why is it that in Western societies like in Europe and America the cases of hypertension, strokes, heart attacks, insomnia, psychological disorders etc. are on the rise while blood pressure, for example, in tribal ethnicities doesn't even increase with age?

Sports are recommended by any Doctor and surely improves blood circulation, lung capacity etc. but there is a **big difference between sports and movement**.

For example, professional athletes that produce tons of **Endorphins**, actually risk "athlete's depression" which is caused by the abstinence from the Endorphins, that build tolerance and are needed in increasingly greater quantities by the body in order to have the same effect. Even if "sports stars" were to release their most profound tension, they wouldn't come to the neurotic behaviors and psychological stress that we know to exist in public figures.

"Sunday athletes" often stress their bodies for the whole week as they are closed in an office. Daily athletes go to the gym after work and say they it makes them feel better. In fact, they do enjoy a few hours of Endorphins and in the long term Serotonin, but never enough to stop stuffing themselves the rest of the time.

I'll note that the human body, like that of animals, is not designed to move on command, but according to its needs that originally coincided with a goal, if not God would have given us wheels.

In brief you could say that the release of tension in humans must always go through a social "censure" that doesn't allow him to enact his animal part. Even those in war torn countries who are socially "enabled" to release stress through violence, don't seem to receive psychological benefits from it if not in those 5 minutes of killing someone with a machine gun. That means that **he really isn't releasing anything**, given that the next day, like our bulimia example, he is at square one again.

Conclusion: you cannot release tension if it must be contemplated by the conscious thought, that in some way takes account of the Limbic System and therefore inhibits animal release. **Does this mean that Humans can't release tension**? No, it means that they require particular conditions: one certainly can't control a voluntary release **while at the same time inhibiting it** for known reasons. Everyone, as adults, has experienced at least once (aside from when we were little and there was no control) a time where our defense were not quick enough to inhibit the release, and notice that it is always in hostile situations. One example is in the case of an emergency that doesn't allow you time to think, and only afterwards you released what you've done. Don't worry, that isn't automatism, but release, since automatism implies the same inhibition. The problem would be what happens afterwards; in general, as I mentioned, we quickly get sucked into social conditioning. This means that even afterwards, some stimuli, that we will see later should still be present, but easily identifiable with the animal kingdom in mind. Naturally, you can skip the resistances and release under the influence of psychoactive substances, but the next day there is another problem: other than the resistances that rearrange themselves, we might have to deal with an addition to the substance.

5.3.6.2 So what do we do?

Let's go back to Pet Therapy. Say I put a neurotic subject on a deserted island full of animals that growl and murmur from morning to night. At the beginning, the subject will feel extremely uncomfortable, perceiving them as "dangerous." Slowly, however, given that in the end, he too is an animal, he will start to "howl." He will realize that for the other animals, it could be a sign, and it won't take long for him to understand when and when not to do it, but this does not take away from the fact that even if it is for example, an expression of rage and will have a thousand ways to release it though muscle movements.

Back to the studio: Does it make a difference if we find ourselves with a Therapist with a shirt and tie, with a tidy desk etc. or with one with his feet up that whistles and yawns every now and then? The more you are inhibited, the more the latter will bother you and the more the first will put you at ease. The problem is that the **first** one simply confirms the necessity to be inhibited and will depress your vital animal part but regardless you'll say "but it's comforting." The **second** upsets your civilized part a bit, but the animal part is quite pleased because it sees the opportunity to liberate itself. **So**? The usual lecture: if you're not in contact with your animal part, you **won't know how to manage** the degree of "animality" that your Impatient can handle and therefore you'll scare him away within the first five minutes. Vice versa, over time (depending on the state of the Impatient) the Impatient will start to release tension too, not so much to please you- because pleasing people is only for the civilized part, not for the animal part- because deep down, he also has the same need. Obviously with children that haven't yet been completely inhibited it doesn't take long. With adults it can sometimes take years, but in the meantime they will start to say things like "you know, the other day I reacted to something but I only realized what I'd done afterwards!"

5.3.6.3 The Human fear of "animal" or "bestial" release

It's the primary concern of Humans, trying to disassociate and create distance between the ruthless and cruel "animal" part within us; as if wars, persecutions, the domination of peoples, the ruin of the ecosystem etc. **had been the work of animals** and not Humans (just to its clear that those who make trouble are following the Limbic part, not the animal part). It's funny: they seem like those who oppose gay marriage and adoption with the excuse that it would destroy human society, as if the damage hadn't already been done by heterosexuals and the children of heterosexuals... who knows.

It might be worth remembering that in the animal kingdom, aggressive release never comes without a price (aside from Human pets, what a coincidence), but is always in line with the objective of survival. They have to earn something tangible from it, if they don't change tactic. **For Humans on the other hand**, who rely on their good old evolved Limbic System, all of the frustrations of their childhood become **disproportional reactions in reality**. A Human is capable of shooting another human just because he got cut off at a traffic light, without earning anything from it and believing in that second of fury, that he might "cathartically" resolve what happened in the past, as if the usual bulimia would be resolved once and for all by eating an Elephant

Humans, not only for aggressiveness but for all of the fundamental emotions, should always "measure things out," distinguishing between what reality demands and what the Limbic System's interpretation of reality demands, which is the **real difference between Human and animal behavior, that are only apparently similar**. If they seem like just words to you, think of how much "unprofitable" hate towards certain races, religions, ideologies etc. there is. With the resources we spend on war, we would have had enough to eat for the whole world, so don't say that they were done to ensure the survival of one people that demanded the annihilation of another. They just needed and continue to vent, amplifying a control of bulimic power, that in the long run will bring ruin even to those in control.

In the same way, the main fear of parents, in my experience, is always the same: " but if I teach my son/daughter to release tension like an animal, then he/she will become a beast that doesn't know how to act in society, he'll burp at the table." Mistake... a sense of limit is not engraved in small children by repeating to them ten thousand times that "you don't do that" or giving him a spanking, but my calmly taking him and leading him towards the thing that is dangerous or "inconvenient" to do, just to make him feel the **strength** of your arms as you lift him up. This is the only way he will **internalize a sense of limit** that will then be applied to everything. I'll remind you that threatening children, is a sport exclusive to Humans, regardless of the fact that it has been known for years to do nothing but offer him a behavior model that has nothing to do with survival, and ensure that he will mimic that behavior again in his adult life, reducing his possibilities of channeling anger towards something profitable like creating the conditions for economic survival (something that is increasingly difficult today).

In fact, no one has ever seen an animal beat her pups; she moves them, or stops them without being aggressive. Even adult animals know when to complain or let off steam and when not to because of the context. But rest assured that they release tension even just by moving in a certain way or grinding their teeth alone.

Putting your feet up at a restaurant, would be like for a Lion to roar in front of a much bigger Lion. It's a stupid move, and the animal (and our animal part) **is not an idiot; while the other part is.**

In our culture if you run when faced with someone bigger than you, you're a coward. In the animal kingdom, you're a fool if you don't.

5.3.7   Differed vs immediate release

What difference is there between the civilized Humans and a wild animals attempt to release (aside from our Limbic 3.0 that asks for justice from the past)? **The postponement, or rather the time that passes between the tense stimulus and the release of it.** In other words: the wild animal (or the newborn), doesn't make time between the tension and the pursuit of release. It doesn't wait for it to be after 5pm, for when it can finally go to the gym, a screaming match with their partner, to take it out on someone inferior to them or whatever corporeal discipline you like. Now we even have things like "Zoo total body" that consists of making animal movements to obtain wellbeing (release tension). Not even here are they very concerned with the stimulus, and not the execution of the release. It's as if a child woke up during a nightmare and you told them what to do to shake it off. It might make sense to take small children to the Zoo (a terrifying place) because after a while they would naturally start to play with the animals, **but you can't tell them "how" because it would be unnatural.** If you took an adult, promising him that it will increase his wellbeing, he'd fall for it immediately, doing all of the exercises you tell him to, with careful attention to do them correctly, reinforcing his controlling part, and in the end, getting worse.

The (false) postponement of Humans release that, in that moment inhibits or freezes him, accumulating for hours, days or even years, leads to: 1) Energy that in the meantime takes other Psychosomatic paths (for example a big headache or a spike in blood pressure) that people often take medication for; 2) The unexpressed energy conditions the perception of events that are sequentially between tension and release (for example an overly crowded bus that becomes unbearable); 3) When I release (or think I do), the day after, with my corporeal discipline, the "old" energy will have already taken other paths and I only release a small part of it, and I end up like in the bulimia example: yesterday I didn't eat (release), which caused tension and now I'm stuffing myself. After the indigestion, I'm still tense and again comes the hunger. **Why? Because if someone punches me in the face, the tension (fear, anger) comes immediately and because in order to keep it from fermenting I have to get rid of it as quickly as possible. Silly example: if my parquet gets flooded, I either dry it right away or the wood absorbs the water and swells (and if that isn't clear enough I should just open up an ice cream shop).**

5.3.7.1 <u>So what do we do?</u>

Hoping that it's clear that while an animal releases stress every second of the day for whatever distress, Humans, for reasons we examined earlier, accumulate it, now, what do we do with the Impatient?

First of all, as I mentioned, it makes a difference if the Therapist is as stiff as a ski boot or as loose as a goose. The signal that the patient receives in the first case is to be good and keep their mouth shut. **It makes even more of a difference** if the Therapist (or the discipline) believes to be able to "defer" an emotion that's been blocked for some time, because, as mentioned, by now the water in the parquet has already been absorbed and now you want to mop it up.

What does it take to dry up parquet that has already been impregnated with water? **Heat** (of the sun or a radiator).

What does that mean for the Impatient? If he starts to shorten the time between stimulus and release, even for the tiniest instances of tension, he'll create a "heating system" that with time, will dry up the "parquet." Example: if an Impatient tells you that today someone stole his car, it would be enough for you to "roar." It seems like nonsense, but try going to a monkey, even one in captivity, and playing with it for an hour, giving it nuts and taking them away. Sure enough after a few a while you'll start making noises and gestures as well. With small children it doesn't take long, they immediately synchronize with this animal part. With adults, as usual, you'll have to "feel" what level of provocation, the rational or civilized part is able to handle. In the next paragraph I'll use Parkour as an example in order to demonstrate how many little releases of tension create "heating" for the parquet that eventually absorbs the past. You'll be able to tell by their ever more lively and colorful expressions, other than words based solely on reality, without any useless chatter of the mind.

To whoever argues that reacting in an instinctual way is counterproductive (and I'm not talking about automatisms) I would say that there is a fundamental misunderstanding, and that is thinking that in the animal kingdom is ruled by "here and now the objective" while in reality is ruled by **"here and now the expression or movement that releases energy and tension."** The motor expression of release and displeasure is not meant to directly obtain "the thing" but is means of itself that allows to keep excess energy low in order to have a view of reality that consents it to know when to wait for the right moment to act.

It is thought that animals don't have the **patience and tolerance for frustration,** and yet it is exactly the **opposite**, its Humans that don't. In the first, release is useful precisely for increasing tolerance; in the latter, release (or rather acting impulsively, believing to release instinctively) means the illusion of achieving a goal immediately, dictated by prior experiences or automatisms, when in reality the exact same thing done a million times always requires adequate adaptation, because the conditions are never exactly the same (I'll remind you that automatism is often the main reason for accidents).

Handling frustration, knowing how to wait, **shouldn't be the fruit of emotional inhibitions of the past such as "just keep quiet and deal with it,"** but of the **continual release of small tensions**, that allow you to wait until the action takes place at the best possible time to achieve success.

The uncontrolled release of the mind (or better, the Limbic System) **is scary**. Everyone thinks of punching someone in the face and then ending up in jail or worse, **but animals don't do this**, only Humans do (because of the usual Limbic). When you have nightmares, or in other words when the Limbic System and the animal part start quarreling, the consequent release is much more that of the animal than of the Limbic (guess why). Unsurprisingly any Psychiatrist will tell you that a good night sleep is the best cure, allowing you to "reset." But what does that mean? That it releases the conflict by deleting it, like when you reset your phone when it's stuck.

What is happening to sleep in increasingly significant measures? That it's become a problem, because it means abandoning control, and giving it up to "internal monsters." The result' increase in the consumption of pharmaceuticals (or natural remedies, another big business) to induce it.

5.3.7.2 <u>An example of Psychotherapy of Nature: Parkour in Gaza</u>

I won't bother telling you what Parkour is and how it was born, you can find that on the internet. Here I would like to show you how it is **used as a form of Natural Psychotherapy, that is of free release**. Obviously given you've had a minimum amount of primary nurturance, otherwise you won't even get your shoes on. On the **Gaza Strip**, there are a few kids that, without consciously knowing it, take part in a sort of Animal Psychotherapy, freeing the body through movements that come naturally. They aren't preparing for the Olympics or training with other athletes in a stereotypical way, but they jump and hop through ruins as if they were warriors that need to capture a prey, and therefore do not aim for a perfect and "narcissistic" execution but look more like an animal chasing after its prize.

These kids release tension how, when and for however long their body wants to, and without interfering, because it activates the most archaic survival systems and therefore, without being too contradictory, and regardless of their geographical limits, are more free and vital than we are.

I read various interviews with these kids and they all say the same thing, using different words: **"I can't imagine a future for myself, we live under siege. This is the only way we have to feel free."**

Even for them however, the **attractive Sirens of civilization** are getting closer. Today you can find them on YouTube, a few of them founded the "Gaza Parkour Team" (they take tourists around while doing tricks), they are making themselves known in the world and are careful about what they do on camera. They have t-shirts with writing on them, they are trying to "sell themselves" to "our world". From a liberating movement, it's becoming a mind-controlled movement (such as that of athletes). They want to change their conditions survive, have access to clean water and food, and rightly so, but they should know that the price to pay for joining civilization is the loss of vitality, neurosis and depression. I don't know for how much longer, but here is their slogan: **"Despite the <u>pain</u>, there is hope**." Why did I underline "pain"? An animal would already know, it is inescapable, but I'll get there later on.

5.3.8 Laughter as involuntary release

After having passed the first half of my life in the world of show business (first doing stand-up to pay for my studies and then as an author to quickly buy a house) I would add a few notes about laughter, even in therapy, as a mediator between our civilized part and our animal part. In fact, laughter allows for an involuntary release of tension (other than producing endogenous endorphins), thus releasing a minimal amount of tension and dribbling the resistances.

Unsurprisingly Psychology of Humor does exist, and studies the psychological and biological effects of laughter in addition to its underlying mechanisms.

Now, obviously don't expect a depressed Impatient to be very willing to laugh, but once again, I'll let you imagine what it's like to have a therapist before you with a stick up their ass, compared to having one that crosses the line every now and then, in a good way and at the right time, in order to make you laugh. On the internet you'll find loads of information on humor, even before Freud's theory of humor of 1905, but as I said, don't expect much. It is impossible to free oneself so easily from such profound psychological cages. If one went to read about the presence of humor and laughter in Impatients with strong psychological disorders, they would be quite disappointed.

Frankly, I don't even believe in certain types of "Laughter Therapy," that add the voluntary act of "forcing" oneself to laugh as an exercise three times a day after meals. Pretty much, it is a small thing that allows for release in neurotics, that allows our animal part to "breath" a little bit.

5.3.9   Give stimuli, not solutions

We already know about the vice of those in the field of Human psychological wellbeing (official and non), of "**doing**" something to "**make him better.**" We sure do deserve some goddamn satisfaction after all the years we spent studying! More than a few times, Impatients have come to me saying that their prior therapist had told them that they couldn't do much because "he" didn't want to change. You'd think at least one would answer back saying "good job, moron, that's why I came here," but no, they just took it home with them.

It's something greater than us. It seems like if the anxiety of not being in control doesn't take over, and **Humans' interventionist practices are renowned even in politics**, many electors prefer someone that says "Hi, I'm going to do something completely ridiculous" rather than one that placidly affirms "I dunno, let's have a good look at the situation and then figure out what to do."

Our animal part doesn't do that. I've never seen a *"Sarchiapone"* ("Sarchiapone" is a fictional animal, used during a tv sketch by Walter Chiari, a famous Italian tv performer) that says to his pup "no, in the *Sarchiapone* manual it doesn't say to move like that, but like this." **The animal is patient and waits for its pups to grow, stimulating them and not giving them pre-packaged responses. The point isn't even to make them realize when the answer is correct, but to make them move freely (protected, in the beginning). When they move, the answer can be found on their own, they just need to observe.**

5.3.9.1 So what do we do?

There are a thousand ways, that I clearly won't tell you, to stimulate the animal part of a Human adult, even in a studio, but you'll get there on your own if you really think about what your average Wolf would do with its pups, or think of the stimuli that a fetus has in the womb, or when just born. Think of the dark, the sounds, the sense of touch, the odors- you can play with and stimulate reflexes, reactions etc.

The important thing, as I mentioned, is that you continue to be in contact with your animal part in order to know the usual "how, when, for how long's etc." **Breathing and free movement are a consequence of nurturance, not the other way around. And when you are old enough, life itself give your nurturance,** or rather nature gives us limits and at the same time the possibility to roll around like children within those limits. To obsess over anything or one is a deviation caused by our neurosis, because in nature we are all connected to the world. The only healthy dependence we should have is on life itself, **everything else is just experience that must never block our vitality.**

5.3.10 <u>The Limbic resistance (to change)</u>

As mentioned previously, the Limbic System (intended more symbolically in this case rather than as an exact Neurophysiological reference) is the one that opposes resistance to change. It is the emotional and motivational center of insatiable desire for both the revenge of childhood frustration and the need for the loving - but "civilized"- nurturance of parents, that will then lead us to feel empathy towards others as adults. **In other words**: it doesn't want to change because surrendering to and giving up revenge, that is having "things" that reward us, would lead to **depression**- but it is the only way to free oneself from the trap. If someone kicked your ass 30 years ago, you can take it out on as many people as you want, but the wound remains, and you only waste your life by constantly looking for the best shoes to kick with and the most adequate asses to kick. **Furthermore, the Limbic System** is afraid to change, because if you free yourself from the trap, you are psychologically **disobeying** your parents who might be dead and you're 60 years old and their ghosts are living inside of you. You're afraid of **losing their love** that, as an adult you will transform in other facades, ideologies, beliefs, loves and blah blah blah.

Therefore, since the Ego (the rational and conscious part of the persona) also and **especially takes orders from the Limbic**, in the form of "emotions that push you to…," the first level of resistances can be explained by the Impatient himself, perhaps with the usual "you don't understand how I am, there are certain things I would never do" etc.

Then, there is a **second, more profound level** of resistance that appears in dreams, in certain psychiatric disorders that is obviously more distressing because it fears **punishment** for disobedience etc.

5.3.10.1 So what do we do?

I've said this, but I'll repeat myself with the metaphor about the Wolf I took away from Siberia. If after two years I send him back to live with the other Wolves, do you think he wouldn't resist (for fear of not being able to survive or being abandoned by his peers) even though his animal part, having been civilized with me, is unhappy and depressed?

The only thing I can do is gradually expose him, under my protection, to his peers. **Therefore, as a therapist**, I have to **simultaneously expose** him to my animal part (if I haven't also repressed mine) and reassure his civilized part with mine.

What this does is allow the resistance to slowly fade away: the Impatient realizes that surrendering to his animal part won't provoke real catastrophes, that is he won't go around attacking people if it isn't for his own survival (going back to the world of Hillman), and neither will he be attacked by me or the ghosts of his oppressive parents who are no longer there. Furthermore, the fear of losing the support of his ghost-parents- unconsciously present even though they aren't actually there to tell him what to do, that resemble a typical husband-wife container of false nurturance etc.- **begins to be replaced by the certainties of Mother Wolf, that is the animal Therapist, that raises you and then lets you free.**

In effect, if someone wanted a step-by-step formula, it would be like asking a Wolf what exactly it is that they do. I could tell you that in my clinical experience it is sometimes like playing a game, but to tell the truth, it is much more simple and at the same time complex. All it is body language, including facial expressions, a prosody, a few breaks and looks that change every second, according to the state of the Impatient, just as a Horse would in Pet Therapy. **In addition, there is the Therapist** that must remember that there is also a civilized part of the patient that must be reassured by the civilized part of the Therapist (which is actually false, but the Impatient won't find that out for a while). **The Therapist must therefore acquire the right tools**, something that made my mentor, a greatly accomplished Psychoanalyst rumble, for example when I told him that with particularly dependent patients, the (obviously more expensive) added possibility of texting in the nurturance or matronage phase was extremely effective. Don't think they'll bombard you with messages, they just need to know you're there and over time they'll need it less and less. **The important thing is never to do**

anything in disaccord with the Impatient's contract, that's "collusion." If the sitting is supposed to last 50 minutes and something comes up at the last minute, causing the sitting to be prolonged by 3 minutes, that delay needs to be announced, because a Mother Wolf must be clear about when it's time for one thing or another.

5.3.11 The heart of the question: Endorphins

We all know (and if you don't, there's Wikipedia) what Neurotransmitters are and how much they influence our mood. Here I'm referring more to **Endogenous Opioids** (produced by our body) rather than Serotonin, Dopamine, Adrenaline, Noradrenaline etc. that in synthesis regulate our mood, but in such a complex way that it would be better to limit ourselves to saying that ideal life conditions allow us to regulate many things.

So let's take the more immediate **Endorphins** that we all know (it would be more interesting to talk about Endomorphins 1 and 2, but you can look that up). **Their function in nature is that they are produced in case of pain and/or exhaustion, and to "reward"** us for appropriate behavior, such as while mating. **Simply put, they are needed to improve the probability of survival of the species.** It is obvious then, that **substances similar to Endogenous Endorphins exist,** not only in Humans but even in **so-called "inferior" animals.**

We aren't interested, if not for specific examples, in **Exogenous Opioids** (those not produced by our own body); substances derived from Alkaloids such as Heroin or synthetic pharmaceuticals that both replace the Endogenous Endorphins in our receptors.

The main point is that both exogenous and endogenous endorphins cause **addictions**, meaning that they are capable of **influencing our behaviors** with the goal of obtaining more and more. What's more, such substances build **tolerance**: the more time passes, the greater quantity necessary to obtain the same emotional wellbeing. So, if you aren't able to handle the **little abstinence crisis' that they provoke, you become something of a "junkie," that doesn't seek or see anything other than a way to get it, excluding the abstinence crisis or mini depression.**

Naturally, objects and people are capable of producing such endogenous substances, and thus they can also "offer themselves" to Humans so that they don't care for anything but them. Do you want a list of everything they can "offer"? Everything that I've mentioned in this book concerning "false nurturance," from the last cell phone model to whatever belief of indispensable promise of some charismatic "savior," to our illusions of love that stir up great emotions but then collide with reality.

From these few lines you can comprehend Primitive or Natural Psychotherapy in its entirety and how Human has been controlled during the civilization process, in the sense that their animal part has been put to sleep, *that* is the answer to Hillman and Ventura regarding why professionals (and amateurs) of psychological wellbeing **have lost sight of the outside world: they were too worried about finding Endorphins for their own receptors.**

5.3.11.1 <u>Why don't animals ever become "junkies"?</u>

Even animals release Endorphins and some species, at certain times, resort to **psychoactive substances found in nature** (exogenous) that, other pain and stress relief, can be used for their various positive collateral effects, such as disintoxication.

It's obvious however, that animals don't abuse these substances, if they did there would be four dominant ones and loads of prey too busy with getting "a fix" as in the case of Humans. **Why** don't animals (wild ones) become "addicted" neither to endogenous nor exogenous endorphins?

It's written between the lines: because they are always and inevitably in contact with **pain, fear, exhaustion etc., weapons given to them by nature to protect themselves and survive, that allow them to act with constant awareness of what is happening on the outside.** Vital doesn't necessarily mean happy, but "feeling" all of these perceptions (if you don't like to consider "pain" an emotion) necessary for survival that cause both pleasure and displeasure.

Animals go through a cycle of pleasure and displeasure, and that is why they never become addicted, and if they do it's because it is actually convenient to them and their survival, and not without reason like we do. Going back to the usual case of the Wolf pup, he might be dependent on the Mother Wolf, that causes him to produce lots of nice Endorphins, but since she has no interest in not letting him grow and keeping him with her forever, she grants him the freedom to experiment on his own, so that the Endorphins can be produced as nature intended. This makes him free and-attention- immune to blackmail from anyone and anything (unlike us) that makes him produce "distinctive" Endorphins because he knows that even if you get kicked out of "Paradise," after a while his good old Endorphins will be there to cheer him up. What does he do in the **meantime**? **He wails his pain away**, he **"unloads" tension, a trick of nature necessary to tolerate pain (abstinence) while waiting for "reinforcements."**

To whoever thinks that if I were to offer a wild animal some pain relievers in exchange for his liberty… try bringing some Heroin to a Tiger every day, maybe one might hooked, but the others will quickly understand that it isn't worth it.

In Humans, you can see the effect of natural liberation of Endorphins, after every war, for example the World Wars, where physical suffering had awoken our animal resources and thus our Endorphins, that allowed us to go back to reality and see it as completely useless in terms of survival of the species, but merely as an expression of what it really is: an act of dictated dominance characterized by delirious greed that attempts to tame depressive voids. Unfortunately, once peace established, the game of avoiding the unpleasable sensations of absence of Endorphins begins once again and "dealers" are always in abundance.

5.3.11.2 The "abstinence crisis" of the Endorphins of civilization

The heart of the question is that we are so used to believing we are in control of everything, that we end up avoiding the pain/distress- the kind we cannot control, but that has been managed for millions of years by our animal part- of a "crisis" induced by the absence of Endorphinic "products" that civilization offers us and we become trapped.

I'll remind you that there is a form of depression that matures, that needs to be experienced. If I don't surrender to the loss of any old thing, I will be dependent on whatever image of that thing that is offered to me. It's like the famous "5 stages of grief" if you will, but it's always been more talked about than felt, because otherwise the effects would be seen in the protest of Human-animals against the subtraction of the environment and therefore in the maturing of the Humans race.

There are situations however, that at times cannot be avoided by escaping and finding refuging in Endorphins perhaps found in alcohol, cigarettes etc. For example, when we are unwell for health reasons, in this case we cannot control the pain, not even with medication- **and *that's* when it becomes clear to everyone that this book is completely useless**. You might, in this case, see all of our bodily functions come back to life, shouting and thrashing about until our natural Endorphins come around to calm us down, even as we wait on our death bed.

Hospitals would be like "screaming houses" if it weren't for the medicine that interrupts this process; and if it is true that we artificially prolong our lives, on the other hand we also distance ourselves from our animal "instinct," that contains profound suffering but also profound joy, **one cannot be without the other**. It is impossible to have only the first, if not in the form of some incomplete mental agitation that leaves the other part unsatisfied.

I still believe however that we have not matured enough (and I'm the first to admit it myself). It is useless to use forced willpower to resist, it's better to take medicine, it means already being a bit more mature and surrendering to our limits.

The truth is that if you were never properly nurtured, your Endorphins completely depend on external nurturance, and that's why the world is getting worse. The less you've been nurtured, the less psychologically ready you are to abandon yourself to a **crisis of abstinence from Endorphins**. Unfortunately, the **vast majority of the population** is attached to something, and that is how the **economic**

industry thrives, "drugging us" with a false nurturance that doesn't help us grow. Give me a TV or a Smartphone with internet, but don't leave me alone with the risk of an abstinence crisis.

Going back to Hillman, I believe that the only ones that should act as a real "incubator" are Psychotherapists, the problem is that in order to do his job he should be a "**Mother Wolf**" (meaning not another Endorphin-dependent of our society), and if the Psychotherapy "fails" it is because **he wasn't and continues not to be**. Many of them have fallen for it, so as not to feel real suffering, taking Endorphins from "dealers," perhaps in the form of fame and success.

5.3.12 What about Psychiatric Impatients?

Why do certain communities work? That is, how do they achieve improvements that are sensitive to Impatients that have surely had a very disturbed upbringing that lead to the Psychiatric problem? But most importantly, why are they usually ones that require a return to physical work in an environment in close contact with nature work? **You already know why, it is only a longer path to recovery and as always, one life is never enough, but it's better than never having spent an afternoon in the sun.**

5.4 THE RECOVERY OF THE ANIMAL PART OF THE THERAPIST

Now we'll have a bit of fun looking at the load of work that we will have to do as Therapists, in order to be "revolutionary" a là Hillman, who probably wouldn't really agree, but I don't think he'll read this book, for a variety of reasons, but the most important being that he has been dead for a while now.

I hope it is clear that the "incubator" function of a Therapist **will never have the same strength** on a 20-year-old Impatient than the original nurturance would have had when he was 1. Just imagine if the patient is 50. I myself, as an Impatient (I was one for 20 years) must simply forget about trying to reach my "animal" center and getting rid of the neurosis that civilization brings upon us- not even 10 lives in the jungle would be enough for that. **Hence the conversation shifts** to: up until what point am I willing to live like this, or would I rather finish my life getting as close as possible to my animal part, and as "naked" as mother nature made me. Clearly, given my profession, I chose (and it's not really you to choose but your animal part that is always yearning for more air) to go back to being a "nudist."

So, the fundamental premise for getting closer to our animal part, is that there must be a minimum of functionality that a certain level of nurturance allows for. If there isn't or if it is scarce, the only thing to do is to go to a **therapist that is well-integrated** with his animal part, that nurtures you as if he were the famous "incubator" **until** you have at least some degree of "legs" to walk on, even with 1,000 fears.

Having said this, and since there are different realities, where **regardless of a mediocre nurturance**, a Human is able to- **without becoming a Limbic bulimic** like certain Leaders of the past and present – **rejoin, if only a little bit, with themselves**, perhaps by leaving everything behind (although I don't think that's necessary) and adopting a more "primitive" lifestyle (you'll find many of these cases on the internet).

Now I'll explain how the example of Parkour in Gaza is not the only existing case, of recovering, at least a little bit, our animal part, in order to live not as a "junkie" but with the capability of perceiving what happens around us and dying in peace. Happiness.

I will start with extreme examples just to get the point across, to then come down to things that anyone can do – but in particular those who work in Human psychological wellbeing- to come a bit closer to our vital part, the animal one, that allows us to "raise" other Humans without denying them their essential (animal) part that nature gave us, to then sober up and come back into contact with the real world, but not as they show it to us, not as a "junkie."

As I mentioned, recovering our animal part means, **money-wise**, letting our antique Biology manage the crisis of

abstinence from Endorphins, letting it simmer until our "Ego" stops flopping about in fear of losing control. **Anyway, you can rest assured that with our civility, the loss of control can never be complete**, if not we would most likely end up mangled under a truck the next day. Simply put, don't make a scene about things that are substantially useless.

5.4.1 <u>Example 1</u>

What did Ulysses do when he encountered the sirens (exogenous Endorphins)? He tied himself to a tree to resist them, but this is only a literary example. In fact, it is a **voluntary** (though initial) **act** of the civilized Ego and that is why it **goes on to become part of all of the disciplines that have attempted to cure the Human**, ironically in the most **absurd** way: telling him without telling him to use willpower to "adjust" the enemy of willpower. It would be like trying to cure a Muslim by forcing him to become Christian, a Homosexual to become Heterosexual, raising a Tiger well by capturing it, telling the Devil to be good etc. **Basically, telling my animal part that it must civilize itself for the good of Humanity, when the great trouble of Humanity is all my fault.**

Alas, the techniques based on omnipotent acts of will are immensely popular, even though they clearly don't work. But we know that **the more one suffers, the more they go to wizards** who, with just the flick of a wand…

Let's move on to techniques without willpower then, like the **oriental traditions** that consist in touching the passive body, stimulating anything from Serotonin to Coca-Cola. **Why don't they work** (It doesn't seem like Eastern society is a great ad for the wellbeing of Humans)**? Because it's a downhill, not uphill, solution,** just like anti-depressants-when you stop taking them you're exactly where you were to begin with before taking them, worse even, since in the meantime whatever was rotting inside of you continues to do so.

Note: I am in favor of Pharmaceuticals, especially when the problem keeps you from sleeping or holding a steady job, the important thing is to "survive," so to speak…

Ulysses is an interesting example however, because you can replace the willing act of tying oneself to a tree with real life circumstances that force you to face the crisis of abstinence, and once that was overcome, you would certainly be more animal-like than before, regaining Endorphins. But let's move on.

5.4.2 <u>Example 2</u>

Let's pass to an example where very little willpower is needed. Do you know what Vincenzo Muccioli, founder of San Patrignano (a community dedicated to the

rehabilitation of drug addicts), did with Heroin addicts? He tied them up to radiators in a basement (whether this is true or not does not matter). Ethics aside, and without considering his sanity or lack thereof, we understand what happened: the heroin addicts had to face an extreme crisis of abstinence. They shrieked like eagles, they fought, they suffered… nothing like your typical "exercise" for wellbeing. After ten or so days however, their endogenous Endorphins came about, taking back their place in their receptors, **freeing the addicts of the slavery of external addiction** (Heroin, exogenous). Obviously this did not solve the basic problem of addiction, which stems from a lack of basic nurturance, it is hard to find an addict that didn't seek refuge in other, less damaging sources, but what interests us here is just one thing: **if you don't have a way out, the animal in you shows itself.** Perhaps that was a bit too cruel of an example, I might not sleep tonight… let's take it down a notch.

5.4.3 <u>Example 3</u>

Sailing is a hobby of mine, I've had the luck to witness what happens to some people when they can't see the coast anymore (those who aren't used to it, obviously). **They don't know how sick or uncomfortable they'll feel, therefore it is not an act of will.** They just find themselves in a situation in which the waves are getting bigger and the closest coast is 60 miles away (at least 12 hours of navigating, if all goes well). Some will start to vomit and have no means of escape-

I can only try to make them feel safe, but I can't stop the boat nor turn back around if the sea and wind are going against me. What to do? Bandages are useless if you don't put them on beforehand and there is almost never a good doctor on board to knock them out with a nice tranquilizer. No Endorphins, sorry! **So what happens? The more civilized they were, the more they suffered.** The more animal-like they were, the more likely they were to let themselves go, adapting to the new situation and becoming reborn with a nice charge of Endorphins. Even the most "civilized" of men however, after slowly passing from the hysteria of "let me off!" would end up cursing this and cursing that and so on. Sure, if the sea had been calm before the panic triggered the abstinence crisis, he would have thought twice about doing something like that again, and would go back home to his false securities. **I'm not sure if the similarity is clear: when there is no way out in the middle of the sea, as in life, it isn't that you surrender to your body, but it is your body to take control of you and quiet your mind, becoming an animal. But if a helicopter arrives first and saves you from that boat** (or whatever distressful situation), **suggesting to come back to civilization but only if you promise to stay good and quiet in front of a television or a cell phone for the rest of your life, you'd accept immediately. However, if the helicopter arrives after you've already calmed down and your Endorphins are back in action, and you're eating again, believe me, you would refuse the ride they offered you.**

5.4.4   Example 4

Let's stay seaside, since it gives the right idea and is a great possibility for raising awareness (and I don't mean on a luxurious cruise). My Mentor (Marco Tommasi) is someone that has done nearly everything on a boat, getting himself into unknown circumstances, certainly not like the sailors connected via satellite, with GPS, radar and weather forecasts. All he needed was the stars, a sextant and a few maps. This is because he was the son of sailors with strong traditions, who, in order to guess where the port was, gathered sand from the seabed and tasted it. In fact, of the many "Mentors" that I've had (although for the first 19 years my only mentor was Mother Nature), he was the only one that was able to make himself understood without speaking. He didn't tell you what to do, he would only protect you and let you be, until you synchronized and started to regain your sense of "smell" and sense how the wind blew. In other words, my mentor was a Horse (no worries, he won't be offended).

If you want to know more about these Humans that thought very little and felt very much, I'll recommend a book that was given to me by Marco, written by Riccardo "Dino" Brizzi, a once well-known Neurosurgeon that is almost completely unheard of now, whose passion for the sea led him to study these maritime communities made up of fishermen that he himself described as "primitive." The book can still be found on the internet and is called "*Quando si navigava con i trabaccoli*" (Panozzo Editore, 1999), meaning "when we sailed with *trabaccoli*," referring to a type of sailboat typical of the Adriatic region. The book contains the "Treaty of the Trabaccoli" which was printed for the first time in 1969 (I don't know if there is an English version). A small excerpt to get an idea:

"*... the old men live on the sea, immersed the in the atmosphere around them, and since it depends on their very lives, they are soothsayers. They read the skies like we read books, "they feel" the stride of the boat as they sleep, they wake with the slightest change of wind or inclination, they rush to the deck without being called for, predict damages and readily prepare for them...*"

Can you imagine what it means to set sail with "animals" of the sort? I'm not talking about extreme situations of counterphobic survival to hide and overcome fear, which can be harmful give that it also protects us, but of a "Pet Therapy" of the civilized Humans with a Human-animal. The more time you spend with them, the more you'll become aware like they are and withstand bad weather (or distress) without so much as blinking. Our senses and perceptions are silenced (therefore their responses are suitable to reality) in our modern society. I remember one of the few documented cases of **Enfant Savage** (children abandoned in the jungle and adopted by animals): Amala and Kamala, found in India in 1920 and adopted by Wolves. When they were taken from the Wolves (who had been killed) the two girls walked on all fours, had remarkable vision in the dark and their sense of smell was much more developed than the average Human's. This is to say that we all have a **necessary animal** inside of us, to perceive what is happening on the outside and thus to act in the most appropriate way in order to be free and alive, even without (especially without) someone or something that **buys out our soul**, making us believe that we would never survive without them or it.

5.4.5 Example 5

In everyday life, even in chaotic Metropolis', you'll notice that there isn't an hour, even minute, that passes in which you don't do something" Endorphinic" or "depression-repressing." I could name a thousand of them: snacking, checking to see if you've received a message, thinking about something that happened or will happen or that you desire, turning on the radio/stereo/television etc. It's as if we don't enjoy whatever we're doing at that moment, like small children do before we ruin them, they play using their bodies while pretending to play with something else. It's as if we have to constantly fill the voids with external things. **Translated**: the anxiety of the void (not supported by Endorphins) creates distress and therefore we have to "call" someone or something that eases this distress (essentially something Endorphinic). Or you could always go to the gym to lift weights, run, swim and command your body to make those efforts that result in blessed Endorphin production (or Serotonin, in the long term) that make us feel good at for a couple of hours, at least until the next mini crisis that we resolve with a cell phone App. But have you ever seen farmers from the back in the day (not the ones that drive tractors with headphones on), spading the land, touching clusters of grapes, smelling the tomatoes etc.? They look a lot more like those children that play using their bodies. What's the difference? The children and farmers from the example produce Endorphins in small cycles, with itty bitty abstinence crisis' in between that they get used to without getting anxiety or the need to call the social ambulance. **As for everyone else**, as soon as they get a little anxious or have the slightest Endorphinic crisis, they rush neurotically to fill up the void, that for a few minutes alleviates the "displeasure," knowing that the next minute they'll find something else, becoming slaves.

What did I say? That we have the opportunity to get closer to our animal part every minute of the day, you just need to "**taste**" the little void that we feel before lighting a cigarette or eating a piece of chocolate, and then not light the cigarette or eat the chocolate. You can do the tiniest things, dosing them out as you wish. This distress, even if it only lasts for a millisecond before stuffing yourself with a doughnut, is a millisecond that will bring you that much closer to your animal part. **Naturally**, as I said, small children, animals, farmers (let's call them "**primitives**" in this sense) accompany distress (that is, they express it) though sound and movement, without raising their blood pressure.

Warning nr.1) this has nothing to do with willpower. There is willpower when, anxiously, I check Messenger, but if I don't, my "Ego" gets sucked in by the "distress" that comes from somewhere else I can't control, that chops up my "Ego." In fact, willpower is needed to come out of the uncomfortable sensation by calling someone. It is no surprise that in our advanced societies we use terms like "fight cancer," "combat depression" etc. that is, fighting whatever is not controllable by the Ego.

But when animals are sick or getting old or finish their life's "mission" (like the Antechinus or male Bees after mating), they don't fight themselves, they just go to die somewhere and I don't believe there are Pheasants that, on their death bed, call priests or hunters to forgive. Some believe that animals don't have a conscious of death, which is funny... they are perfectly conscious of physical fatigue, the risks of combat, but not of death? Perhaps they escape from predators that chase them down for fear of getting mugged? I suppose anything's possible.

Warning nr. 2) don't believe that in order to let your animal part live in a Metropolis you have to go around doing Parkour between skyscrapers or scratching your ass when you're out in public. **Personally**, now I find myself just making faces, whining like a Goat... they often tell me that after having cultivated so many interests, that all the obsessive, rigid and determined willpower cost me a lot. **Not at all**, and I even grew up in public housing with 6 people living in 45 square meters and at age 13 they sent me to work in the afternoon after studying in the morning. Ok, but what jobs did I do? All manual work: errand boy of the vinter, mover, painter, unloader at the fish market, gardener... I was basically a pack horse.

What's the trick when I feel like everything is falling to pieces and haven't gotten anything done, and the only thing I see the couple of bucks I have in the bank (my prey)? **The trick is in the release of tension**. My parents, farmers transplanted in the city "in search of fortune," still made use of their expressive part later on. My father continued gardening even if he was a Taxi driver, he was nearly inseparable from his spade and the earth. My mother had these unforgettable shopping bags, and made different noises as the number of bags she carried went up. I'm writing this damn book, but don't think I'm sitting here crouched over in front of the computer, every now and then I find myself in ironed out positions (the word "stretching" would ruin the pleasure) that are never the same. I experience them, I don't do them.

Do you think I do such things **in front of Impatients**? (with a few, just something to unconsciously stimulate them, but only when the time is right and if they can handle it). The rest of the time, **I've always done my "Parkour" on my own time and without ever breaking a nail**. Unsurprisingly, my first love was corporeal psychotherapy, but then I didn't like much that they wanted to "teach a cat how to climb," something I've never really *known* how to do myself- I just do it. De

Andrè, a famous Italian singer, once said: "know before understanding" which says a lot.

I don't need to tell you at a certain age you start to deal with deaths, divorces, **but for this book's purposes**, (that's already starting to break my balls, but I think it's in our DNA to leave our experience to those to come) **it's good to know that even in a jail cell or in a concentration camp** (my Uncle was so well trained that he came back to Italy from Germany by foot, after the Second World War, he died while working a sedentary job in the city) **if the free body dies, you will die soon after, and so will your body.**

6 CONCLUSIONS

Good news: Primitive or Natural Psychotherapy **has lost**, if you intend it as an attempt to reinstate adequate life conditions for living beings on earth.

To quote Freud again, perhaps now you'll understand when I say that all this didn't just happen yesterday, but much earlier: *"The liberty of the individual is not a benefit of culture. It was greatest before any culture...Liberty has undergone restrictions through the evolution of civilization."* where "Liberty" can easily be replaced with "Vitality."

The prodigious mind, that executes the work of the delirious Limbic omnipotence that constantly requires more power because it is never really satisfied (blaming our animal part which has nothing to do with it) now has the means, even "falsely democratic" ones that have reduced us to fruit flies on a windshield, all they have to do is turn on the wipers. We have **to fight them with their own weapons**, using our analytic part, but the risk of ending up like them would be very high, especially if before doing something like that we aren't integrated with our healthy animal part that is inclined towards the real survival of itself and the environment.

Hitler's idea was perfect; it was that of a real jungle animal whose life is being taken- he just had the wrong objective. What he should have done was eliminate all of the dickheads preventing the survival of the human race and the planet itself, not the Jews. So really he had to eliminate himself first, since only dickheads get their objective wrong. **OK, STOP HERE AND CLOSE THE BOOK FOR A MINUTE...Reopen it and consider how angry or scandalized you were after reading such a thing. Good, it's a little test to measure the distance between your Limbic (that you only sense with your mind) and your animal part; the more bothered you are by what I wrote, insulting me or hating me for it, the greater the distance. Why?** Because that is exactly how an animal would reason: anyone who prevents my survival gets eliminated, period. An animal wouldn't do anything but take back all of the resources for survival we took away from it- he wouldn't spare anyone, including me since I have central heating and a car, and just because of that, though indirectly, many would be eliminated. There wouldn't be the problem of understanding who the dickheads were, they would be easy to spot: any attack on the survival of anyone else or on the planet, that means I would be among them too, damn it. 'Too late', 'I'm sorry' or 'thank goodness'- I'm not sure. Furthermore, (and now they'll accuse me of promoting delinquency) a legitimate defense is valid only if someone tries to kill me in that very moment, if I shoot him a second before nothing would happen. But if someone tries to kill me in a few years, by giving me cancer by means of radiated foods, various types of pollution or ridding me of my sanity because the money I've made has gone towards making someone else richer- everything changes; if I shoot him, they give me a life sentence and in some places the electric chair, and that would almost be comical, because it would be as if

"the law permits homicide only for direct, not deferred defense" was written somewhere. Every attempt of revolution is now considered terrorism, and every sort of terrorism is now financed and technologically supported by us Westerners that have a handful of naïve fanatics controlling the world.

There is no going back, because although people don't know it, we are already in the pre-panic phase, so much so that never before has it been so simple to make someone believe or sell someone something with the promise of wellbeing- the famous "false Endorphinic nurturance" that turns us all into junkies in search of a "fix" that have an increasing sense of distress without knowing the reason for it. Our animal part has all the answers but is in (or has been put in) a coma, because of its danger to those who want to do business. This desperate search for solutions are convenient to the economic powers (who control politics, which doesn't exist) because they keep the people busy "looking for fixes" and help keep the market flowing.

Today they use the **most beloved Leader of the people** to get them to accept the finishing touches for people control, other than fingerprints, Apps, Google and Facebook, who already own all of our data, we would even be willing to put a microchip under our skin for our own safety against "terrorism." Everything is going just swell, they've even gotten rid of that bothersome thing called winter, thanks to climate change and a little more sun will life our spirits as we wait for cancer to get us.

Do you see what all of the conquests and progress of Humans was for? They were nothing but a prelude or the foundation of all of this. Let it be clear that I'm not a Jehovah's witness declaring the end of the world, but worse! For many of us the world has already ended: because of work, physical and psychological health, bursts of immigration (as if they were coming from Mars, they're only coming because we starved them). Thanks to the Media, these "terrible" things end up like dust under the carpet, but not for long. Be careful however that we are near the end: immigration will increase and will weaken Europe and the United States, bringing with them new consumers capable of working 13 hours a day in order to consume, something that us Westerners no longer know how to do. It's a shame that the planet isn't able to support a new massive load of consumer objects obtained through dirty and irreversible energy. Now even the oceans are safe: there are increasingly less fish and more sicknesses, but the swimmer doesn't realize it until he's swimming in black water.

What does the culture of psychological wellbeing mean when we have radioactive waste in our building foundations because they don't know where to put it anymore? They should have created warriors ready to fight and defend the "territory" first of all, and in a very broad sense, because psychological wellbeing cannot exclude a vital "space." **Even so**, we are full of promoters of self-empowerment, Counselors, Coaches in every field, PNL experts, Psychologists of all sorts, Psychotherapists etc... we should all be feeling better but in reality **all of the data shows the**

complete opposite: deterioration of the personal and professional sphere.

Why is that? As I said in other words, there are **two ways** of "curing" distress: **the first** is that of false Endorphinic nurturance that makes you feel like part of something or someone, but doesn't allow you to see reality and therefore to create anything real (curing your sickness by drugging you); the **second** is that one that wakes you up and lets you see how things really are, paying the price of pain and suffering but the only real way to make changes. If you're not hurting, then you don't take your hand off the fire, period. It's **useless** to do a course in Marketing in a country where people don't even have eyes for crying, all it's for is taking the rest of what they have from them.

These "curative" figures have always existed, though under another name, and over time they have become more and more of the first type. There were once philosophers, and before them herders, and even before them those without names, who only prepared their young to face the environment independently, to survive. Only a few made it, but they were used to reality, not the nurturance they never had, they accepted what they had, whether things went well or went badly, exactly like in the animal kingdom of our origins.

No animal has ever put anything before the first command, that is: trying to survive, while seeking the right conditions, whether it goes well or not is not a given, but in order to do that you must have been shown reality, and it couldn't have been by someone who hasn't seen it themselves.

I'll repeat that there is never bad faith, only ambivalence. In the Limbic System there is both empathy and bulimia of possessing useless things in order to dominate. When defeated, even the most evil of dictators cries, convinced of being misunderstood, unless he is really psychopathic. **In the meantime, the world is still going on about "good guys and bad guys,"** and the bad guys are believed to be our animal part (or the beast within us, as they say). If we were all just Boars, the world, aside from meteorites, would go on forever. Only Humans have managed to make a dump of the future in all possible ways, and many are already suffering because of it, but time is running out and soon, with the help of robots it'll only take a thousand people to make the world go round, but they'll live wearing gasmasks and lead armor to protect themselves from the radiation.

The price of liberty, as I've said, is very high. If you don't let be the greatest work of engineering- that Humans, with their analytic intelligence will ever understand- that is our Biological or animal part, you end up attacking yourself. That means, and I'll say it for the last time, surrendering to the fact that our little heads are good for doing times tables, but in order to live a vital and wise life, preserving not just our own but that of the next generations, we must let go of the bulimia of the Limbic System (or however you want to call it) and embrace the animal part, that knows when it is satisfied and goes hand in hand with the fear and suffering that prevents it from doing foolish things. Many people tell me: "but I'm in so much pain, I just want to die." If it isn't clear, **there are also two kinds of suffering: the first** is that of the Ego, of rationality, the conscious of our civilized part. It suffers because it doesn't give up. It's missing "endorphins" and thus makes a fuss about getting the pharmaceutical, person or "thing" without which it can't live without. Be aware that this has nothing to do with the newborn baby that calls his mother to relieve itself, what I'm talking about is just the neurotic adult version of this request for nurturance that, by the way, pushes us right into the trap of being at the mercy of Endorphin "dealers." The second kind, is the one that, when you can't do anything and you know you just have to deal with the situation. When you give up and your mind goes blank, to give space to physical pain, that knows what to do in order to attempt survival, but the vital kind, not the plastic kind. It is with this second "suffering" with which animals and wise Humans coexist, that allows for liberty and is a necessary phase, or rather a presence that, if constant in our lives, would solve the problem of endorphin "dealers" because they would no longer have any clients. Even the sane warrior, like an animal, doesn't go into battle without fear (which is already pain); he needs it to protect himself. Only when Humans overcome fear are they sure to crash.

Conclusion: after all this, we can only choose whether to die tripping, dancing, making love while somersaulting or to cozy up to our coffin with our new Tablet. Those who have genes so powerful that they age like an animal, will see the alienated people that will be left in this "Blade Runner," dragging their oxygen tank behind them and screwing maniacs, but they won't be angry, just pleased to have died free of self-conflict.

And with that I'd say I've happily concluded my business as a writer on "*Psicognagnola.*" (ED: Italian slang used by my mom, meaning someone that complains about petty things, so as not to address more serious problems) I now continue on my "primitive" path because I prefer to be among the lowest ranking in the animal hierarchy than the highest among Humans. That's all for now, bye bye! ☺

About the author

As my good friend Doctor Rosy Gagliardo says (whose résumé I could write another book on), I was "sequentially monothemed" meaning that I've liked the same "things" since I was five years old, things that went on to become my life: whatever was going on inside the heads of my relatives (there were six of us, I was the youngest), humor (never lacking in my house), writing lame songs (thanks to my brother who played music), water and wind (the family lake house at Como, Italy).

That's all, love doesn't count because everyone believes it's the soundtrack to their own life.

Table of contest